浙江省社科联社科普及课题成果（17ZC01）

INSIDE CHARACTERISTIC TOWNS
OF ZHEJIANG PROVINCE

# 走进浙江特色小镇

王利华 著

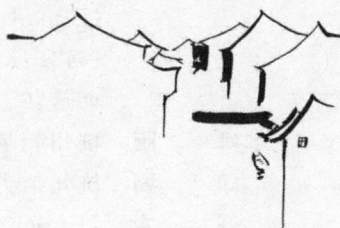

**Hangzhou**
**杭 州**

Southern Yuhuang Mountain Fund Town
上城玉皇山南基金小镇

Ding Lan Wisdom Town
江干丁兰智慧小镇

The West Lake Wisdom Town
西湖云栖小镇

The West Lake Yunqi Town
西湖云栖小镇

The West Lake Longwu Tea Town
西湖龙坞茶镇

Yuhang Dream Town
余杭梦想小镇

Yuhang E-Fashion Town
余杭艺尚小镇

Fuyang Silicon Valley Town
富阳硅谷小镇

Tonglu Health Town
桐庐健康小镇

Lin'an Cloud Manufacturing Town

浙江工商大學出版社
ZHEJIANG GONGSHANG UNIVERSITY PRESS

**图书在版编目(CIP)数据**

走进浙江特色小镇 / 王利华著. —杭州:浙江工
商大学出版社,2017.6

ISBN 978-7-5178-2216-5

Ⅰ. ①走… Ⅱ. ①王… Ⅲ. ①小城镇－概况－浙江
Ⅳ. ①K925.55

中国版本图书馆 CIP 数据核字(2017)第 111363 号

## 走进浙江特色小镇

王利华 著

| | |
|---|---|
| **责任编辑** | 王 英 罗丁瑞 |
| **封面设计** | 林朦朦 |
| **责任印制** | 包建辉 |
| **出版发行** | 浙江工商大学出版社 |
| | (杭州市教工路 198 号 邮政编码 310012) |
| | (E-mail:zjgsupress@163.com) |
| | (网址:http://www.zjgsupress.com) |
| | 电话:0571-88904980,88831806(传真) |
| **排 版** | 杭州朝曦图文设计有限公司 |
| **印 刷** | 杭州恒力通印务有限公司 |
| **开 本** | 710mm×1000mm 1/16 |
| **印 张** | 16.5 |
| **字 数** | 210 千 |
| **版 印 次** | 2017 年 6 月第 1 版 2017 年 6 月第 1 次印刷 |
| **书 号** | ISBN 978-7-5178-2216-5 |
| **定 价** | 45.00 元 |

**版权所有 翻印必究 印装差错 负责调换**

浙江工商大学出版社营销部邮购电话 0571-88904970

# Illustration

## 插　图

# Zhejiang's Characteristic Towns—Geographical Distribution

**Huzhou city**

Huzhou Silk Town
Huzhou Writing Brush Town in Shanlian
Deqing Geographical Information Town

**Hangzhou city**

Southern Yuhuang Mountain Fund Town in Shangcheng District
Ding Lan Wisdom Town in Jianggan District
The West Lake Yunqi Town
The West Lake Longwu Tea Town
Yuhang Dream Town
Yuhang E-Fashion Town
Fuyang Silicon Valley Town
Tonglu Health Town
Lin'an Cloud Manufacturing Town

**Jinhua city**

Yiwu Silk Road Financial Town
Wuyi Hot Spring Town
Pan'an Medicinal Herb Town

**Quzhou city**

Longyou Mahogany Town
Changshan Stone Appreciation Town
Kaihua Root Carving Town

**Lishui city**

Liandu Ancient Weir and Painting Town
Longquan Celadon Town
Qingtian Stone Carving Town
Jingning She Group Town

**Jiaxing city**

Nanhu Fund Town
Jiashan Sweet Town of Chocolates
Haiyan Nuclear Power Town
Haining Fashionable Leather Town
Tongxiang Fashionable Sweater Town

**Ningbo city**

Jiangbei Power Town
Meishan Marine Financial Town
Fenghua Coastal Health Town

**Shaoxing city**

Yuecheng Rice Wine Town
Zhuji Sock–Art Town

**Taizhou city**

Huangyan Intelligent Mould Town
Luqiao Volvo Town
Xianju Natural Oxygen Bar Town

**Wenzhou city**

Ouhai Fashion Manufacturing Town
Cangnan Taiwanese Town

(来源:《科学 24 小时》2016 年第 78 期;绘图:乐园,制图:张凯)

# 浙江省第一批省级特色小镇分布图

**湖州**
- 湖州丝绸小镇
- 南浔善琏湖笔小镇
- 德清地理信息小镇

**杭州**
- 上城玉皇山南基金小镇
- 江干丁兰智慧小镇
- 西湖云栖小镇
- 西湖龙坞茶镇
- 余杭梦想小镇
- 余杭艺尚小镇
- 富阳硅谷小镇
- 桐庐健康小镇
- 临安云制造小镇

**金华**
- 义乌丝路金融小镇
- 武义温泉小镇
- 磐安江南药镇

**衢州**
- 龙游红木小镇
- 常山赏石小镇
- 开化根缘小镇

**丽水**
- 莲都古堰画乡小镇
- 龙泉青瓷小镇
- 青田石雕小镇
- 景宁畲乡小镇

嘉兴
南湖基金小镇
嘉善巧克力甜蜜小镇
海盐核电小镇
海宁皮革时尚小镇
桐乡毛衫时尚小镇

宁波
江北动力小镇
梅山海洋金融小镇
奉化滨海养生小镇

绍兴
越城黄酒小镇
诸暨袜艺小镇

台州
黄岩智能模具小镇
路桥沃尔沃小镇
仙居神仙氧吧小镇

温州
瓯海时尚智造小镇
苍南台商小镇

(来源:《科学 24 小时》2016 年第 78 期;绘图:乐园,制图:张凯)

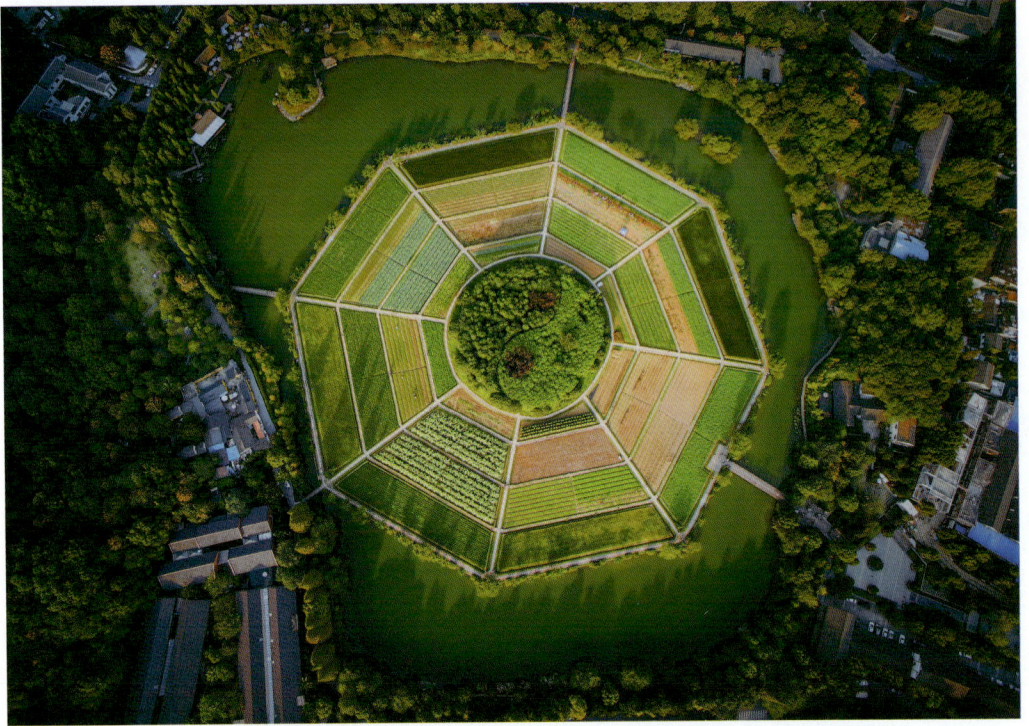

Southern Yuhuang Mountain Fund Town in Shangcheng District

Ding Lan Wisdom Town in Jianggan District

The West Lake Yunqi Town

The West Lake Longwu Tea Town

Yuhang Dream Town

Yuhang E-Fashion Town

Fuyang Silicon Valley Town

Tonglu Health Town

Lin' an Cloud Manufacturing Town

Jiangbei Power Town

Meishan Marine Financial Town

Ouhai Fashion Manufacturing Town

Fenghua Coastal Health Town

Cangnan Taiwanese Town

Huzhou Silk Town

Huzhou Writing Brush Town in Shanlian

Deqing Geographical Information Town

Nanhu Fund Town

Jiashan Sweet Town of Chocolates

Haiyan Nuclear Power Town

Tongxiang Fashionable Sweater Town

Haining Fashionable Leather Town

Yuecheng Rice Wine Town

Zhuji Sock-Art Town

Yiwu Silk Road Financial Town

Wuyi Hot Spring Town

Pan'an Medicinal Herb Town

Longyou Mahogany Town

Kaihua Root Carving Town

Changshan Stone Appreciation Town

Huangyan Intelligent Mould Town

Luqiao Volvo Town

Xianju Natural Oxygen Bar Town

Longquan Celadon Town

Qingtian Stone Carving Town

Liandu Ancient Weir and Painting Town

Jingning She Group Town

# Introduction

Zhejiang is known as a province that is "seven-tenths mountains, with two fields and one water." In the new economic norm, it is a problem for Zhejiang to further optimize the productivity layout in such a limited space. However, the foreign development models such as "Switzerland's Davos Town" "The United States Greenwich Town" and "French Provence Town" inspired Zhejiang. Although these towns are small in size, they are very delicate and unique. With low-density buildings and a vital economy, these towns present ecological charm. In order to crack the bottleneck of space resources, promote industrial transformation, and improve the living environment, the Zhejiang provincial government issued Guidelines on Accelerating the Planning and Construction of Characteristic Towns in April, 2015, proposing to cultivate 100 characteristic towns in three years. On June 4, 2015, the first Zhejiang Province Characteristic Towns were officially announced, and 37 towns from 10 cities were included in the first list as followed.

Hangzhou City (9): Southern Yuhuang Mountain Fund Town in Shangcheng District, Ding Lan Wisdom Town in Jianggan District, The West Lake Yunqi Town, The West Lake Longwu Tea Town, Yuhang Dream Town, Yuhang E-Fashion Town, Fuyang Silicon Valley Town, Tonglu Health Town, Lin'an Cloud Manufacturing Town;

Ningbo City (3): Jiangbei Power Town, Meishan Marine Financial Town, Fenghua Coastal Health Town;

Wenzhou City (2): Ouhai Fashion Manufacturing Town, Cangnan Taiwanese Town;

Huzhou City (3): Huzhou Silk Town, Huzhou Writing Brush Town in Shanlian, Deqing Geographical Information Town;

Jiaxing City (5): Nanhu Fund Town, Jiashan Sweet Town of Chocolates, Haiyan Nuclear Power Town, Haining Fashionable Leather Town, Tongxiang Fashionable Sweater Town;

Shaoxing City (2): Yuecheng Rice Wine Town, Zhuji Sock-Art Town;

Jinhua City (3): Yiwu Silk Road Financial Town, Wuyi Hot Spring Town, Pan'an Medicinal Herb Town;

Quzhou City (3): Longyou Mahogany Town, Changshan Stone Appreciation Town, Kaihua Root Carving Town;

Taizhou City (3): Huangyan Intelligent Mould Town, Luqiao Volvo Town, Xianju Natural Oxygen Bar Town;

Lishui City (4): Liandu Ancient Weir and Painting Town, Longquan Celadon Town, Qingtian Stone Carving Town, Jingning She Group Town.

What is the Characteristic Town exactly? The Characteristic Town is based on a characteristic industry, bringing together relevant organizations, institutions and personnel to form a modern community with a distinctive and cultural atmosphere. Specifically, the Characteristic Town is not a "town" in the traditional sense. Although independent of the urban area, it is not an administrative division. The Characteristic Town is not an "area" in a regional development process either. It's different from the industrial park and tourism park. The Characteristic Town is much less a simple overlay of industries or functions, which is not its essence. In fact, the Characteristic Town is based on information economy, environmental protection, health, tourism, fashion, finance, high-end equipment manufacturing and other industries to create a distinctive industrial ecosystem, in order to promote the local economic and social development. It even plays a certain role in the surrounding areas, as a new impetus and innovation carrier in the regional economic development. From the connotative view, the Characteristic Town has four characteristics: a "special and strong" industry, an "organic" function, a "small and beautiful" appearance and a "new and alive" mechanism.

Zhejiang's characteristic towns, though their geographical area maybe less than that of half of the West Lake, carry great innovative and developed strategies, which practices new governance concepts of the Central Party Committee. They promotes the coordinated development of urban and rural areas, and simulates the development of new industrialization, urbanization and agricultural modernization, thus strengthens the development potential in the weak areas, strives to form a balanced development structure and continuously enhances the whole development.

Today in a number of characteristic towns, these new platforms, lying in the junction of urban and rural areas, integrate industrial ecology and natural environment, and get community functions and tourism services readily available, like a unique Jiangnan painting gradually drawn into the town. These new communities become enviable places for living and work. This is not only Zhejiang's great innovation move，but also its overwhelming strategy.

# 前　言

　　浙江素有"七山一水两分田"之说。在经济新常态下,如何在非常有限的空间里进一步优化生产力布局,是浙江面临的问题。瑞士的达沃斯小镇、美国的格林威治小镇、法国的普罗旺斯小镇等发展模式让浙江受到启发。虽然这些小镇空间体量都不大,但造型十分精致独特,建筑密度低,产业有特色,经济富活力,文化具韵味,生态多魅力。为破解空间资源瓶颈、促进产业转型升级、改善人居环境,2015 年 4 月,浙江省政府出台《关于加快特色小镇规划建设的指导意见》,提出用 3 年时间重点培育和规划建设 100 个左右的特色小镇。2015 年 6 月 4 日,浙江省第一批省级特色小镇创建名单正式公布,全省 10 个设区市的 37 个小镇列入首批创建名单。

　　杭州市(9 个):上城玉皇山南基金小镇、江干丁兰智慧小镇、西湖云栖小镇、西湖龙坞茶镇、余杭梦想小镇、余杭艺尚小镇、富阳硅谷小镇、桐庐健康小镇、临安云制造小镇;

　　宁波市(3 个):江北动力小镇、梅山海洋金融小镇、奉化滨海养生小镇;

　　温州市(2 个):瓯海时尚制造小镇、苍南台商小镇;

　　湖州市(3 个):湖州丝绸小镇、南浔善琏湖笔小镇、德清地理信息小镇;

　　嘉兴市(5 个):南湖基金小镇、嘉善巧克力甜蜜小镇、海盐核电小镇、海宁皮革时尚小镇、桐乡毛衫时尚小镇;

　　绍兴市(2 个):越城黄酒小镇、诸暨袜艺小镇;

　　金华市(3 个):义乌丝路金融小镇、武义温泉小镇、磐安江南药镇;

　　衢州市(3 个):龙游红木小镇、常山赏石小镇、开化根缘小镇;

　　台州市(3 个):黄岩智能模具小镇、路桥沃尔沃小镇、仙居神仙氧吧小镇；

丽水市(4个)：莲都古堰画乡小镇、龙泉青瓷小镇、青田石雕小镇、景宁畲乡小镇。

特色小镇到底是什么？特色小镇是以某一特色产业为基础，汇聚相关组织、机构与人员，形成的具有特色与文化氛围的现代化群落。确切地说，特色小镇不是传统意义上的"镇"，它虽然独立于市区，但不是一个行政区划单元；特色小镇也不是地域开发过程中的"区"，有别于工业园区、旅游园区等概念；特色小镇更不是简单的"加"，单纯的产业或者功能叠加，并不是特色小镇的本质。特色小镇以信息经济、环保、健康、旅游、时尚、金融、高端装备制造等产业为基础，打造具有特色的产业生态系统，以此带动当地的经济社会发展，并对周边地区产生一定的辐射作用，是区域经济发展的新动力和创新载体。从特征内涵上看，特色小镇具备四个特征：产业上"特而强"，功能上"有机结合"，形态上"小而美"，机制上"新而活"。

浙江的特色小镇，尽管它们的地域面积可能没有半个西湖大，但小空间承载着创新发展的大战略，践行着党中央治国理政的新理念。它促进了城乡区域协调发展，促进了新型工业化、信息化、城镇化、农业现代化同步发展，在加强薄弱领域中增强发展后劲，着力形成平衡发展结构，不断增强发展整体性。

今天，在多个特色小镇看到，这些处在城乡接合部的新平台，产业生态与自然环境融为一体，社区功能与旅游服务一应俱全，一幅幅独具江南诗画韵味的协调发展画卷在小镇展开。"产、城、人、文"四位一体的新型社区，让在特色小镇工作与生活成为令人羡慕的生存形态。这是浙江的创新之举，也是大手笔之作。

# CONTENTS
## 目　录

**Hangzhou**

杭　州

# Southern Yuhuang Mountain Fund Town in Shangcheng District

Old factory buildings, messy warehouses, abandoned railways, and a large number of indigenous villagers were the original appearance of the approximate 1.3 square kilometers—the Southern Yuhuang Mountain. However, there was a 700-year-old Eight Diagram field, and the beautiful Jiangyangfan Park. It was close to prosperous cities, but far from the hustle and bustle of modern life.

With such a place, people loved and hated it. Hangzhou government racked their brains creating a myth of wealth at Southern Yuhuang Mountain Fund Town, saying it was a place of natural ecology, cultural environment, and an area leading to a path to real economic development. In just a year, the Fund Town has attracted more than 1600 professionals, and more than 80 billion in capital was invested in the real economy, which benefited more than 600 enterprises and involved more than 60 listed companies.

How can the Fund Town develop so successfully? Safe & Rich Venture Capital Co.,Ltd. helps us solve the problem. Signed in July last year and officially settled this year, Safe & Rich Venture Capital Co.,Ltd. moved from the Huanglong business district into Fund

Town. To the staff, the most striking is the Fund Town's office environment, which is a villa-style office building completely different from high-rise ones. A series of great hardware conditions such as a high-speed broadband network, convenient staff canteens, fitness centers, internationalized medical institutions, and educational facilities, which are no worse than those in a Central Business District. Furthermore, services in the town are run to suit the convenience of companies. For example, the newly registered enterprises can receive a license in a working day. Enterprises, after settled, can enjoy "one-stop" services. Banks and a special tax branch offer great convenience for companies to apply for projects, financial support and other services.

Besides a beautiful landscape, high-quality hardware support, and convenient services, the Fund Town have also built a financial ecosystem, linking innovative resources together. "We have a lot of communication with so many financial institutions here." This is how people settled in the town feel. The overall atmosphere of the town here makes it particularly easy to find the right partner. Zhejiang Cybernaut Investment Management Co., Ltd. totally agrees with it. Last year, Cybernaunt invested 3 billion yuan into more than 30 new projects. For example, they cooperated with Hangzhou Kaitai Capital Management Co., Ltd. on an internet game project. "We rarely tried the game and entertainment industry before, but this was what Hangzhou Kaitai Capital

Management Co., Ltd. was familiar with," the CEO of Cybernaunt said. They were surprised to see the appreciation of their investment three months later, after the game company in which they invest was acquired.

At present, the town has nurtured a number of first-class private institutions, attracted provincial government investment, and opened commercial banks for financial services. Compared to Shanghai, the Fund Town not only has a more beautiful environment, but also has better international facilities, more convenient education, medical, and administrative services. It will make full use of these advantages to attract more enterprises to settle down.

# 上城玉皇山南基金小镇

破旧的厂房,凌乱的仓库,废弃的铁路和大量的原住村民,这曾是占地1.3平方千米的南玉皇山原貌。当然,还有700年前的八卦图,美丽的江洋畈公园。这儿毗邻繁华的城市,但远离现代生活的喧嚣。

有了这样一个让人又爱又恨的地方,杭州市上城区政府绞尽脑汁创造出了一个财富神话:玉皇山南基金小镇。这是一个保持自然生态和文化环境的地方,一个开始步入实体经济发展的区域。仅仅一年时间,基金小镇已经聚集了1600多名专业人士,有800多亿资金投入实体经济,受益企业600余家,涉及上市企业60余家。

玉皇山南基金小镇为什么能发展得如此成功?安丰创业投资有限公司落户小镇的过程帮我们解开了疑团。该公司从签约到正式落户只花了半年左右的时间,从黄龙商圈搬进基金小镇,公司员工最满意的是基金小镇的办公环境——独栋别墅式的办公楼与商圈的高楼大厦完全不同;其高速宽带网络、健身中心、工作人员食堂、国际化的医疗机构、教育配套等一系列硬件条件又完全不输 CBD 商务区。此外,小镇还为公司提供专业化服务。小镇行政服务中心实行"五证合一""一照一码",新注册企业可以实现一个工作日领证。企业入驻后更可享受"一站式"服务,不出小镇就有银行。政府还专门成立了税务分支机构,为企业最大程度上做好项目申报、资金扶持对接、银企对接等服务。

除了美丽的山水景观,高品质的硬件支持,便捷的服务,基金小镇还构建了一个"金融生态圈"，并且成为创新资源聚集的纽带。"很多金融机构聚集在这里，我们有很多的沟通交流机会"，这是入驻小镇很多企业负责人的想法和感受。现代商业合作应该是开放的，该小镇的整体氛围让企业很容易找到合适的合作伙伴。关于这一点，浙江赛伯乐投资管理有限公司更有发言权。去年，赛伯乐新增资本 30 亿元，投资了 30 多个新项目。其中，他们与杭州凯泰资本管理有限公司合作，投资了一个互联网游戏项目。"我们很少尝试游戏、文化娱乐产业，而这正是杭州凯泰资本管理有限公司熟悉的领域。"赛伯乐负责人说。没想到三个月之后，这家游戏公司即被并购，一举升值了三倍。

目前，小镇已经集聚了许多一流的私募机构，吸引了省、市政府及部分民间产业母基金落户，吸引了为企业提供融资服务的商业银行。基金小镇不仅拥有更加优美的环境，而且拥有更良好的教育、医疗和行政服务等国际配套设施。玉皇山南基金小镇将充分利用这些优势，吸引更多的基金管理人来投资。

# Ding Lan Wisdom Town in Jianggan District

During the Eastern Han Dynasty, there was a man named Ding Lan, whose parents both died when he was young. He missed his parents so much that he had his parents' statues carved out of wood. He discussed everything with the statues and ate meals before he paid respect for his parents. He spoke to them about where he was going and came back to tell them about his safety. He never became relaxed at the trivial formalities in his life. Since then, the town has become famous for Ding Lan's filial piety. Now, two thousand years have passed. Ding Lan's hometown and other historical traces are still retained, and Ding Lan Town began its gorgeous turn in 2014.

According to the requirements of the Hangzhou Municipal People's Government, Ding Lan Town was listed as the pilot area of Zhejiang Province's "Ecological Intelligent Urbanization Program," becoming the only "Wisdom Town" in Hangzhou. According to the government of Jianggan District, Hangzhou, the overall plan of Intelligent Town is formulated by Tsinghua University. The planned area is 2.5 square kilometers, with a land area of 0.7 square kilometers approximately, which includes the core area of the West Lake Intelligent Industrial Park, the Wisdom Industrial Headquarters, and the Science and

Technology Innovation Park, along with the supporting service industry belt. The town will adhere to the development objective of industry, culture and tourism and promote production, living condition and ecology, striving to build a "leading town" with main ecological environment as the base, business innovation as the core, and cultural attraction as the supporting factor. In general, Ding Lan Wisdom Town has three main features.

Firstly, the people of the town live a smart life. Many people have imagined their future life as a smart life with a variety of automated equipments that are readily available. Many needs in life can be solved with their phones. Now, this kind life has come true in Ding Lan Wisdom Town.

In the town, people at work can check whether the elders' blood pressure at home is normal, whether the children come home from school, or whether the gas is switched off by their phones. When people are not at home, packages can be stored in a beautiful E-mail box, until the tenants pick up them with a password. When people get off work and come back to their communities, the intelligent parking guidance system will soon be able to remind residents where empty parking spaces are. In the evening, after dinner, residents can walk to Gaoting Mountain Scenic Area which not only provides a number of climbing paths, but also installs more than 200 smart contacts, to avoid the "no signal" situation. Residents can enjoy the freshness of nature while experiencing intelligent life.

If the corridor lights do not work, people can just take a photograph and then send it on WeChat, the property management will send maintenance workers at once. In addition, the town establishes a "Monitoring Cloud" to guarantee the town's residential property security, manage the river clearance, the forest protection, and achieve "Integrative Management" and "smart Urban Governance."

Secondly, the town has a culture of filial piety. As the hometown of filial piety, Ding Lan Town has a long history and a strong culture of filial piety. In recent years, the people carried out the election of "Ten Dutiful Child," not only to praise the "filial piety," but also to educate people around the town. The people opened the "Filial Piety Banquet," selected ten specific dishes for the elders, and invited more than 500 people, such as "Ten Dutiful Stars, Ten Moral Models and their relatives" to enjoy the feast. All these activities were in order to spread "Ding Lan Filial Piety" culture. The Ding Lan people also organized various cultural innovation activities about filial piety, which included theme painting, calligraphy sketching, singing and dance, paper cutting, and other works, like the dance "Dowdy Lamp" which was created by the local cultural volunteers who won the Silver Award in the 2013 Zhejiang Province Community Dance Competition. In 2014, the Ding Lan people launched the "Dingqiao Family Tradition" activity. With the chain reaction of "obeying family tradition, innovating the folkway, and promoting social customs," it aimed to create a harmonious and civilized community.

Thirdly, the town has smart parks. Ding Lan Smart Town is composed of three core areas: the West Lake Intelligent Industrial Park, the Wisdom Industrial Headquarters, and the Science and

Technology Innovation Park. The town focuses on e-commerce business and Internet information service, which is appropriate for industries on wisdom and health development, cultural creativity, and business services. Up to now, 89 new enterprises have descended upon the site. 180 thousand people have been received to tour the Gaoting Mountan Scenic Area. It is estimated that by 2017, 500 intelligent enterprises would be introduced to realize a revenue of 1. 8 billion yuan and 180 million yuan of tax revenue, 200 thousand tourists would be received, and 100 senior professionals would be settled there. In addition, the Ding Lan people have also completed the Gaoting Mountain Trail, a cycling road construction, and two natural villages. As the core area of tourism in northern Hangzhou and the last piece of green land in central Hangzhou, Gaoting Mountain Scenic Area was listed as the key ecological construction project in the province in

2013. The total investment was more than 2 billion yuan in five years,

creating the national 4A tourist areas. Since its opening to the public，the Gaoting Mountain Scenic Area has achieved remarkable results，becoming one of the best travel choices of Hangzhou people.

"Between the mountains and green water，the door of wisdom in the Hangzhou's smartest Ding Lan streets has already open." The Ding Lan Wisdom Town is truly becoming an area to gather the "Wisdom of Health" industry demonstration zone，information port，human resources，and ecological beauty.

# 江干丁兰智慧小镇

东汉年间,有一个叫丁兰的男子,自幼父母双亡。他因经常思念父母,所以就用木头刻成父母的雕像。凡事与雕像商议。吃饭之前,敬过父母后自己才食用。出门前告知父母,回来后一定面见,从不懈怠。从那时起,该镇就以丁兰的孝道而闻名。两千年过去了,丁兰故里、丁兰井等历史痕迹依旧留存,但面对一个新世界,丁兰镇在 2014 年开始华丽转身。

作为"美丽杭州示范区·智慧江干"的先行试点,2015 年 6 月,丁兰智慧小镇入选浙江省首批特色小镇创建行列。根据当地政府规划,智慧小镇整体规划方案由清华大学负责制订,小镇规划面积约 2.5 平方千米,规划产业及配套用地面积约 0.7 平方千米,包括西子智慧产业园、智慧企业总部园、科技企业创新园三个智慧园区构成小镇的核心区域,配套城北商业区、皋亭山景区、智慧居住区及临丁路沿线配套服务产业带。小镇坚持"产业、文化、旅游"三位一体和"生产、生活、生态"三生融合的发展目标,推动智慧景区、智慧社区、生活服务业、文化旅游产业协调发展,着力打造以"龙头产业为主、环境生态为基、创业创新为重、文化景区为衬"的特色小镇。总体而言,丁兰智慧小镇有三个主要特色。

第一,小镇具有智慧生活。许多人曾想象未来的生活模样:各种自动化设备随时可用,人们只需动动手指便可满足生活中的众多需求。这种生活状态已经在丁兰小镇里实现。

在智慧小镇,住户不在家也能通过手机随时检查家中老人的血压是否正常,孩子们是否安全回家,煤气开关是否关紧;社区里还安装了漂亮的 E 邮柜,住户不在家时快递可以存放在邮柜里面,待住户回到小区后通过密码开锁、取件;下班回到小区,智能停车诱导系统能很快提醒哪里有空车位;晚餐后,住户可以去皋亭山景区散心。这个"智慧"景区除了可以在游客在登山时,为其智能规划多条登山路径,还将安装 200 多个智慧接点,避免手机无信号的情况发生。游客在骑车登山的酣畅运动中,不仅可以体验大自然的清新,还能享受智慧生活所带来的便捷服务。

平时,如果小区楼道里的灯坏了,居民只要拍一张照片上传到社区服务的公众微信上,物业管理部门就会派出维修人员修理。另外,丁兰街道还在杭州市率先试点智慧安防,建设了"丁兰眼"城市管理联动平台,将治安交警、城市管理、河道水质、森林防火、景区管理、小区物业、移动平台等 510 多个监控探头和感知设备,全部纳入"监控云",实现了一体化的统一管理和智慧城市治理全域覆盖联动管理。

第二,小镇具有孝道文化。作为孝道之乡,丁兰街道自古以来就有悠久的孝文化历史和浓厚的孝文化氛围。近年来,街道开展了"丁兰十大孝子"的评选,不仅是对孝子的褒扬,更是用身边事教育周围的人。同时结合景区建设,开办"孝道养生百家宴",邀请杭州市"孝心百家"、江干区十大孝星、十佳道德模范及其亲属 500 多人共同品尝孝宴,将丁兰孝文化广为传播。在孝文化传承、创新方面,丁兰街道还先后组织了各类包括以"孝"为主题的书画写生、歌舞编排、剪纸等作品创作活动,由本土文化志愿者表演的舞蹈《孝女灯》,还荣获了 2013 年浙江省社区舞蹈比赛银奖。2014 年,丁兰街道开展了"丁桥家风"征集活动,借助"遵家风—带民风—促社风"的连锁效应,实现以文化人、以文聚人,共创"人城共融"的和谐文明新家园。

第三,小镇拥有智慧园区。智慧小镇由三个智慧园区构成:西子智慧产业园、智慧企业总部园、科技企业创新园。小镇的发展以电子商务企业为重点的电商产业集聚中心和软件、互联网等信息服务业企业总部园为主,适度发展智慧健康、文化创意、商业服务等行业。到目前为止,已有89家新企业落户,预计到2017年年底,引进智慧型企业500家,实现营业收入18亿元,税收1.8亿元,接待游客20万人次,集聚中高级人才100名。此外,丁兰街道还完成了皋亭山游步道、骑行道建设和两个自然村风情小镇提升工程。作为杭州北部旅游的核心区、杭州中心城区最后一块绿地,皋亭山风景区于2013年被列为全省重点生态建设项目,五年总投资将超过20亿元,创建全国4A级旅游景区,打造杭州休闲旅游新中心。自皋亭山风景区开门迎客以来,景区取得了显著成绩,参观接待人数达18万人次,成为杭州人最佳出行旅游的选择之一。

"青山绿水之间,杭州城里最'聪明'的丁兰街道,智慧之门已然打开。"丁兰智慧小镇必将真正成为"一区两港三美四融合"的智慧产业集聚地。

# The West Lake Yunqi Town

The West Lake Yunqi Town，located in the core field of Hangzhou Zhijiang National Tourism and Vacation Park，is a beautiful place with Wuyun Mountain and clear waters. The town covers only an area of 3.5 square kilometers，but more than 400 enterprises have settled there by the end of the first half of 2016，which achieved an output value of 3 billion yuan and a revenue of 200 million yuan in 2015.

In 2015, the computing conference was successfully held in Yunqi on October 14th to 15th. More than 21500 participants, 42584 exhibitors, and over 3000 enterprises took part in it. Global participants were developers from powerful IT nations like the United States, India, Israel, and from nations like Lebanon, Venezuela, and the United Arab Emirates. More than 1. 27 million people watched the live television conference while thousands of related articles were published by 300 domestic and foreign media.

Why does this small town have such an impressive magic? What is the reason behind Yunqi town's vital development? Five main features of Yunqi town can answer these questions.

First, there is a group of excellent leaders. Yunqi town has an honorary mayor whose name is Dr. Wang Jian. He is very famous as Alibaba's Chief Technical Official, and Ali Cloud's founder. He is the main creator of Yunqi town, and is committed to constructing the first innovative town in China. Mr. Shi Yigong, another leading figure, is the Vice President of Tsinghua University who initiated the founding of West Lake University in Yunqi town. Another exemplary person is Sun Quan, the current President of Ali Cloud Computing, moved into the town with more than 1000 engineers. These leading figures are like a banner inserted in the ground of Yunqi Town, who lead and inject a number of innovative spirits into the Yunqi Town project.

Second, the town aims at high-end emerging industries with Cloud computing as the core content. The town focuses on building the Cloud industry ecosystem and developing intelligent industrial hardware. During the process of several years' development, it has introduced the most advanced Cloud data known as IDC. In addition, a number of other Cloud computing companies in the cloud business have also been introduced. Now the whole town has formed a relatively complete Cloud eco-industrial chain.

Third, Yunqi Town uses an innovative business mode. "Government dominating, private enterprise leading, entrepreneur as a main body" is the construction model of the town. The "government dominating" section is through our government's building an excellent service system and offering an excellent entrepreneurial environment to attract industries. "Enterprise leading" refers to the introduction of Foxconn, Ali Cloud, Intel, China Aviation Industry and other well-known enterprises, which bring successful experience to Yunqi Town to guide and help small and medium-sized entrepreneurs grow. "Entrepreneur as a main body" is to provide a platform for government and private enterprises in order to meet entrepreneurs' needs, to develop and build an industrial ecosystem, so that every entrepreneur can enjoy the town and achieve their dreams.

The fourth feature is a new industrial ecology. Yunqi Town has built an "innovative ranch, industrial black soil and technological blue sky" innovative ecosystem. The "innovative ranch" is committed to serving small and medium-sized enterprises with Alibaba's Cloud service capabilities, Taobao's internet marketing resources, Foxconn's industrial manufacturing capacity, and other innovative hardware centers to ensure that they become new creators of value. 264 hardware innovation enterprises are participating in it, along with 54 companies who have settled in Yunqi Town, 31 of which are in the bid. "Industrial black soil" is to build the

West Lake Innovative Research Institute, the Internet Engineering Center, etc. Relying on Ali Cloud, Dt Dream, and other large technological companies, it aims to achieve an organic integration of traditional industries and internet entrepreneurial power, to speed up the realization of "Internet Plus."

Last but not the least, there is a world-class computing conference. Yunqi Town has created a conference which truly serves innovation and entrepreneurship. It is currently the world's largest Cloud computing and DT era technology sharing-event. The 2015 Hangzhou Yunqi Conference attracted about 20000 developers around the world, 80% of whom were under 35 years of age. There were well-known experts at home and abroad attending the meeting. They discussed about technological innovation in quantum computing, artificial intelligence, biometrics, and advanced learning. They brought their own projects, and innovative dreams which can really change the world! Alibaba Chairman Jack Ma once said, "Each time I come to Yunqi town, I feel excited and panic. What I am excited about is that I see a real kingdom that we hoped for 15 years ago, and that one day there would be an entrepreneurial boom in China. I feel panic, because every time I hear people speaking about creativity, I almost cannot understand it. I am lucky that I started business twenty years ago, but I simply can not compete with these young people."

The next step is that Yunqi town will closely focus on the characteristics of its connotation, comprehensively improve the quality of its construction, and strive to become a demonstration town in Zhejiang Province.

# 西湖云栖小镇

西湖云栖小镇位于杭州之江国家旅游度假区核心地段,坐落于五云山脚,是一个有山有水有景的美丽地方。小镇规划占地约 3.5 平方千米,2015 年小镇企业实现云产值 30 亿元,财政收入 2 亿元。到 2016 年上半年为止,累计落户企业有 400 余家。

2015 年 10 月 14 日至 15 日,"杭州·云栖大会"在云栖小镇成功举办。参会人员超过 21500 人,参观逾 42584 人次,参展、参与企业 3000 多家。在全球范围内来看,开发者除了来自美国、印度、以色列等 IT 强国之外,也有来自黎巴嫩、委内瑞拉和阿联酋等国家和地区的。这两天全球直播收看人数超过 127 万,300 余家境内外媒体先后发表千余篇报道……作为全国 5 个云计算服务创新发展试点示范城市之一,杭州走在这个领域的前端;而作为这座城市发展云计算产业的排头兵的云栖小镇也走在前端。此次会议辐射全国,影响力遍及世界,已成为云计算领域的世界级盛会。

为什么杭州云栖小镇有如此大的魔力? 小镇经济如此活跃,背后的原因是什么? 发展模式又是怎么样的? 这些问题可以从云栖小镇的五个特点中找到答案。

首先,云栖小镇有一批杰出的领军者。小镇有一位名誉镇长——王坚博士,他是阿里巴巴的首席技术官、阿里云的创始人,也是云栖小镇主要创建者,他一心致力于把云栖小镇打造成中国未来创新的第一镇。其次,在清华大学副校长施一公先生的牵头下,民办型的研究型大学西湖大学落户在云栖小镇;小镇"千人"联谊会的副会长张辉博士,将"千人"联谊会办公室常设机构设在云栖小镇。阿里云现任总裁孙权,带领着阿里云1000多名工程师迁入云栖小镇。这些精英人物、领军人物,像一面面旗帜插在云栖小镇的土地上,带领和感染着一些富有创新精神的创业者加入到小镇来。

第二,云栖小镇的目标是以云计算为核心内容的高端新兴产业。目前该镇致力于建设云产业生态系统和开发智能产业硬件。在几年的发展过程中,引进了当时全国最先进的一个云数据机房——华中云数据IDC,又引进了全球排名第二的云计算公司阿里云计算有限公司,此外,还引进了像富士康、洛可可、数梦工厂等一批分布在云计算的云业务、云开发,包括云服务和移动互联网等各个领域的一批涉云企业,整个小镇形成了较为完善的云生态产业链。

第三,云栖小镇采用了"政府主导、民企引领、创业者为主体"的创新运作模式。"政府主导"就是通过腾笼换鸟、筑巢引凤打造产业空间,集聚产业要素,做优服务体系。"民企引领"是指引进富士康、阿里云、英特尔、中国航空工业等知名企业,同时也将成功企业的成功能力和成功经验输入到云栖小镇中,打造一个为中小创业者服务的平台,带领和帮助中小企业的创业创新。"创业者为主体"就是创业者永远是云栖小镇发展和持续的动力、活力,小镇坚持以创业者的需求为己任,为创业者创造条件,不断地激发和引导创业者的创造能力,让每名创业者都可以在小镇里面尽情地挥洒创意,实现梦想。

第四,云栖小镇有一个全新的产业生态。小镇构建了一个"创新牧场—产业黑土—科技蓝天"的创新生态圈。"创新牧场"是指凭借阿里巴巴的云服务能力,淘宝的网络营销资源,富士康的工业4.0制造能力等核心能力,打造全国唯一的创新服务基础设施,致力于服务互联网创业创新的中小微企业;"产业黑土"则是要建设西湖创新研究院、互联网工程中心等,依托阿里云、数梦工场等有云计算大数据核心技术能力的公司,实现传统产业和互联网创业力量的有机结合,助推传统企业加快实现"互联网+"的梦想;"科技蓝天"指的是在云栖小镇建成一所一流的民办研究型大学——西湖大学。

第五,有一个世界级的云栖会议。云栖小镇创建了真正服务于草根创新创业的云栖大会,它是目前世界上最大的云计算和 DT 时代技术分享盛会。2015 年,"杭州·云栖大会"吸引了全世界的目光,国内外知名专家、涉云创新创业者逾 2 万人参与,其中 80% 以上的报名者是 35 岁以下的年轻人,很多人还不到 20 岁。他们交流展示量子计算、人工智能、生物识别、深度学习等最前沿的科技创新力量。他们带着自家项目来,用创新的梦想改变世界。阿里巴巴董事长马云曾经说:"其实每次来云栖小镇,心里又激动、又恐慌。激动的是我看到在这儿开启了真正的梦想,开启了十五年以前我们那时候希望的中国有一天创业的热潮。恐慌的是我每次来,听很多人讲话,看很多创意,我几乎不懂。幸好我是二十年以前创业,如果现在创业,估计自己都不知道自己在哪里,根本没法跟这些年轻人竞争。"

接下来,云栖小镇将紧紧围绕特色小镇的内涵,全面提升小镇的质量建设,努力把云栖小镇建设成浙江特色小镇的示范镇。

# The West Lake Longwu Tea Town

The West Lake Longwu Tea Town is located in Southwest Hangzhou. It is one of the six emerging scenic spots and an eco-tourism town along the gold tourism line of "three rivers and two lakes". It is surrounded by beautiful natural environment, many historical sites, and green rolling hills such as Wuchao and Qinglong mountains. There are also the picturesque Daqing Valley Eco-Tourism Park, the Western Hill National Forest Park, and the White Dragon Lake Waterfall. Even the first Hangzhou "Sports Leisure Bike Circuit" and "Western Hills National Forest Hiking Route" are in the town. Since ancient times, it has been a good place for hiking in the spring, spending holidays in the summer, admiring Osmanthus trees in the autumn and walking on the thick snow in the winter. However, it is most famous as the largest "The West Lake Longjing Tea producing area," also known as the West Lake Longwu Tea Town.

The West Lake Longwu Tea Town has been rich in tea production long before the well-known Longjing tea. During the tea season, farmers gathered together, picked tea and chatted in the tea garden, which was recorded in Ma Yuandiao's *Heng Mountain Travels* during the Ming Dynasty. At the end of 2016, the town has about 6.9 square kilometers of tea gardens, more than 40 tea production enterprises, five tea professional cooperatives, and a tea trading market with the annual sales of more than 200 million yuan which accounts for more than 60% of all the West Lake Longjing producing areas.

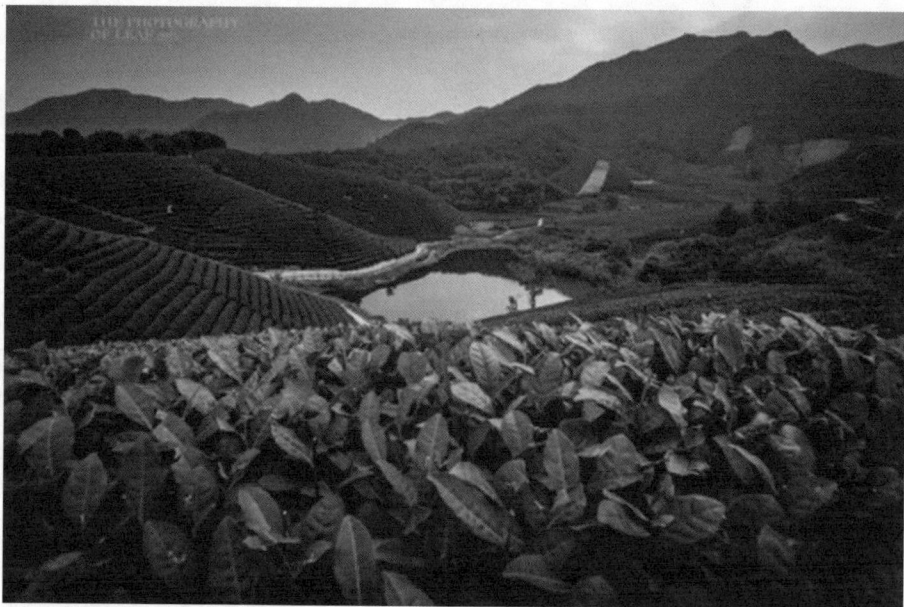

In March, 2015, the Longwu Town started a renovation project, which presented a more beautiful "new appearance." Based on the original ecological environment, it became a rural tourism village with cultural characteristics. It gathered tea gardens, flower gardens, orchards, and vegetable gardens together and made the urban residents return to nature. Here, the visitors can not only drink tea and buy tea, but also understand the tea culture and experience the work of tea farmers. Visiting any tea farmers' home, people can get authentic Longjing tea freely. Choosing a tea restaurant, tourists can see tea parks, enjoying a quiet and peaceful life. In addition, the tea ceremony, fragrance ceremony, yoga, and other related theme activities are carried out from time to time, which brings a new way of life to the Longwu Town.

The West Lake Longwu Tea Town people, from generation to generation, plant tea, fry tea, sip tea, and not only create their own tea ceremony, but also provide outsiders a healthy "paradise."

# 西湖龙坞茶镇

龙坞镇位于杭州市西南侧,是杭州市新兴开发的六大旅游风景区之一,为"三江两湖"黄金旅游线上的一个生态旅游大镇。它三面环山,自然环境优美,历史遗迹众多。它有苍翠连绵的午潮山、小和山、青龙山,风景如画的大清谷生态旅游公园、西山国家森林公园、白龙潭瀑布,更有杭州市第一条"运动休闲自行车赛道"和"西山国家森林徒步登山路线"。自古以来,龙坞镇就是春天踩青、夏天避暑、秋天赏桂、寒冬踏雪的好地方,同时,它还是最大的"西湖龙井茶产地保护区",亦被称为龙坞茶镇。

其实早在龙井闻名之前,龙坞茶镇的十里横山已经盛产茶叶了。在采茶季节,茶农与茶亲聚集在一起,在茶园里劳作、采摘、聊茶,其中的故事,在明代马元调的《横山游记》中早有记载。到2016年末,镇上有约6.9平方千米的茶园,40多家茶叶生产企业,5家茶专业合作社,以及1个茶叶交易市场,年销售茶叶2亿多元,产量占西湖龙井所有产区的60%以上。

从2015年3月起,龙坞茶镇整治工程启动,至2016年7月成功蜕变。小镇在原有的生态环境的基础上,成为具有文化特色的乡村旅游村落,以青山、小溪、茶园、山林、村落为背景,以悠久的茶文化和民俗文化为精髓,集茶园、花园、果园、菜园、庭院于一体,使都市居民回归自然。在这里,游客不仅可以喝茶,买茶,还可以了解茶文化,体验茶农的工作;随意访一户茶农之家,便可"讨"到正宗的龙井茶;随意选一家茶楼,便可面朝茶园,宁静致远。禅茶、茶道、香道、瑜伽等相关主题活动,也会不定期地开展,为龙坞带来了新的生活方式。

龙坞茶镇，一代代茶人在这里种茶、炒茶、品茶，创造属于自己的茶道，也为寻茶而至的外来人，提供了一个健康养生的"世外桃源"。健康养生项目在千年茶镇陆续落地。

# Yuhang Dream Town

Jack Ma once said，"Yuhang is the place where the dream of starting up a business comes true". Located in the west of Hangzhou，there is actually such a place in Yuhang called Yuhang Dream Town. Constructed in September，2014，Yuhang Dream Town officially opened in March，2015. At present，Till now，it has attracted more than 280 entrepreneurship programs，over 2000 talents，and over 30 billion yuan of investment funds.

Why is Dream Town so attractive to people in a short time? Overlooked from a distance，buildings of the Dream Town are like seeds in a field. The most striking ones are 12 big granaries，which are converted from old barns into offices for graduates to begin their business. Every day，an endless stream of people come to the Dream Town to visit and exchange information. The "seed houses" become one of the must-see scenic spots. In front of the granaries，there lay an old street with a history of more than 880 years. On the street stand the ancestral home of Zhang Taiyan and a large number of other ancient buildings. "Here we pay equal attention to the protection of cultural heritage and economic development，" said the Deputy Director. The principle in the Dream Town is that ecology comes first, and production second. Therefore, the harmonious coexistence of human and nature embodies the ecological beauty in the Dream Town.

The Dream Town not only has beautiful scenery, but also is the springboard of entrepreneurs to achieve their dreams. Here, the rent, Wi-Fi, and Cloud platforms are free. There are also convenient dining halls, "U Plus" apartments, and Apple-store-like service halls. A financial company used to help others to sell insurance. Now it has done thousands of online deals after two months in Dream Town and it has pushed out a new Insurance Application. The creativity made it become the first listed company in the town. Zhang Tong, who worked in Alibaba for several years, started to cultivate a musical model with a bunch of young people in the Dream Town. "Many Chinese now want to do new things. It's an honor for me just to try. " said Zhang proudly.

A dream comes from good expectation for the future. Young entrepreneurial groups have dreams, passion, knowledge and creativity. But they have no capital, no experience, no market, and no support. The purpose of the Dream Town is to help young people start from scratch and make their dreams come true. "We are providing rain and sun, while you are responsible for thriving" is the slogan of this ecological and technological town, which provide favorable environment and convenient platforms to young people.

# 余杭梦想小镇

马云曾经说过,余杭是实现创业梦想的地方。在余杭也确实有这样一个地方,它就是梦想小镇。自 2015 年 3 月正式开门迎客以来,梦想小镇共引进 280 多个创业项目,2000 多名创业人才,各类资金超过 300 亿元。

梦想小镇到底凭什么如此吸引人？远眺梦想小镇,各式建筑就像撒在田野里的种子,其中最引人注目的是 12 个大粮仓,这些是由旧谷仓改造而成的办公场地,现在成了许多大学生创业的地方。每天,络绎不绝的人来到梦想小镇参观和交流,"种子仓"成为人们必到的景点之一。在谷仓前,有一条 880 多年历史的古老街道,街上保留了章太炎故居和四无粮仓等大量古建筑。在这里,当地政府高度重视文化保护和经济的协调发展。梦想小镇的开发原则是"生态优先,生产第二"。因此,梦想小镇高度体现了人与自然和谐共处的生态之美。

梦想小镇不仅拥有美丽的风景,更是创业者实现梦想的跳板。在这里,租金是免费的,WIFI、云平台也是免费的。还有方便的大餐厅、"U＋"公寓及为创业者定制的梦想服务大厅。杭州某金融公司原来只是一家帮助别人推销保险的企业,而在入驻梦想小镇两个月后,成功推出了新的保险应用程序,成功完成了数千个网上交易,成为小镇第一家上市公司。在阿里巴巴工作了好几年的张桐,离职后开始在梦想小镇和一批年轻音乐爱好者创办了"蝌蚪音客"。他说:"年轻人应该尝试新的东西,这是一种荣誉。"

梦想,源于对未来的憧憬。年轻创业群体有梦想、激情、知识和创造力,但他们没有资本，没有经验，没有市场，没有支持。梦想小镇的目的就是帮助年轻人从头做起，实现他们的梦想。"我们为您提供阳光雨露，而您负责茁壮成长"，一个针对人才引进、打造良好创业环境和平台的梦想小镇正在形成。

# Yuhang E-Fashion Town

---

The Chinese characters "艺尚" suggest art and fashion（E-Fashion）. In June, 2015, Yuhang E-Fashion Town was selected as one of the first provincial-level towns. The town has attracted a lot of attention from the outstanding fashion designers, fashion biggies, fashion companies of China. 50 garment enterprises settled in this town, more than 10 designer platforms were introduced, and the taxes were increased to 53 million yuan. In March, 2016, the town signed a strategic cooperation agreement with the China Fashion Association and the China Fashion Designers Association. At the same time, it was awarded the innovative demonstration project during the 13th Five-Year Plan in the Chinese apparel industry.

As to fashion, people spontaneously think of places such as Milan, Paris, New York and London, for high-end fashion brands, fashion colleges, and fashion T-stage shows have gathered in these cities. Today, the E-Fashion Town also wants to become one of them. Chen Lianhong, Vice Director of Linping New City Management Committee, is full of confidence, because the town was engraved with fashionable genes long before the Southern Song Dynasty. At that time, Hangzhou influenced the world's fashion with silk culture. Now

Hangzhou's women clothes have grown to an internationally known brand. In fact, among more than its 1200 garment enterprises, 80% of woman's clothing brands are produced from Yuhang.

With the goal of becoming "China's Milan," the current E-Fashion Town has presented the Chinese characteristic shape of "one center and three blocks." "One center" refers to the main part, which is the cultural and artistic center while the "three blocks" are the fashion cultural block, fashion historical block, and fashion artistic block. Among them, about 1700-meter-long fashion cultural block has eight international and domestic, well-known designer platforms and studios. In the historical block, there are 29 quite distinctive southern China residential areas with the white walls and black tiles, courtyards surrounded with green trees, slender bamboos, and bridges, which will be created into an idyllic neighborhood. In addition, its surrounding areas Qiaosi and Jiubao have gathered more than a thousand clothing design and manufacturing enterprises. The adjacent places such as Haining, Tongxiang, Yiwu, Keqiao are treated as the industrial chain resources of the national clothing base. What's more, an area about 19533 square meters of "555 Electric Business Creative Industrial Park" also makes the town's fashion industry chain more complete.

Fashion education and training is another main function of the E-Fashion Town. Since 2015, when the French Fashion Institute, the French Fashion Cooperation Committee, the China Garment Association and the China Fashion Designers Association settled here, a large number of fashion talents have gathered in the town, which has made it become a fashion "talent camp." "The town will open a China

Fashion Education Institute, and the preparatory work has started."
Chen Lianhong said, "The town will cooperate with three
internationally renowned fashion college—New York University
Fashion School, St. Martin's College of the Arts, and Italy Marioni
College." The 2016 Domestic Outstanding Fashion Design Graduate
Competition is one of the activities. Some of the excellent young
people will be fortunate to take part in "College Fashion Week" held
in the United Kingdom.

"China's Milan" is not a illusion. It is estimated that by 2017, the
E-Fashion Town will accomplish a fixed investment of 5 billion yuan.
It will add 350 million yuan tax revenue, and attract 120 travelling
traders, 600 E-Businesses, and about 30000 thousand entrepreneurial
talents.

# 余杭艺尚小镇

"艺尚",顾名思义,表示艺术和时尚。自 2015 年 6 月余杭艺尚小镇被选为首批省级特色小镇起,小镇就吸引了"国字号"时尚设计协会、时尚大咖、时尚企业的关注:50 家服装企业入驻小镇,引进设计师平台 10 余家,新增税收 5300 万元。2016 年 3 月,与中国服装协会、中国服装设计师协会签署了《战略合作协议》,并被其授予中国服装行业"十三五"期间的重点创新示范项目。

提起时尚,人们都会不约而同地想到米兰、纽约、巴黎和伦敦。高端时尚品牌、时尚学院、时尚 T 台表演正在这些城市聚集。今天,余杭艺尚小镇也想成为其中的一员。"成为中国的米兰",这不只是说说而已。当地政府对此满怀信心,因为这个城市在南宋前就拥有时尚的基因。当时,杭州通过丝绸文化影响着世界时尚的发展。如今,杭州女装已经成长为国际知名品牌,而杭州超过 1200 家服装企业中,80% 的女装品牌是在余杭制造的。

目前,小镇"一中心三街区"基本成型,"一中心"是指小镇主体项目文化艺术中心,"三街区"分别是时尚文化街区、时尚历史街区和时尚艺术街区。其中长约 1700 米的时尚文化街区,已引进 8 个国内外知名的设计师平台和工作室;另外,在时尚历史街区 29 幢颇具特色的"江南民居"在细雨中娉婷而立:白墙黛瓦、庭院修竹、小桥流水……这里将被打造成一个创业田园式的街区。其周边地区乔家和九宝已经聚集了 1000 多家服装设计、生产制造企业,临近还有桐乡、海宁、义乌、柯桥等作为全国服装基地产业链资源带。

另外，占地 19533 平方米的"555 电商创意产业园"也让镇上的时尚产业链更加完整。

时尚教育培训是余杭艺尚小镇的又一个主要功能。自 2015 年以来，中法时尚合作委员会、法国时尚学院、中国服装协会、中国服装设计师协会纷纷入驻，大量时尚人才聚集在这个小镇，艺尚小镇成为一个时尚人才大本营。"开设中国时装教育学院，其准备工作已经开始。"其负责人笑着道出了小镇的开放合作和国际梦想，"小镇将与三所国际知名的时尚学院——美国纽约大学时尚学院、英国圣马丁艺术学院和意大利马兰欧尼学院合作。"2016 年国内开展的优秀时装设计毕业生选拔活动就是其中的一个项目，一些优秀的年轻人将很幸运地被送到英国参加在伦敦举行的"大学生时装周"。

艺尚小镇成为"中国米兰"不再是一个幻想。预计到 2017 年年底，余杭艺尚小镇将完成固投 50 亿元，增加税收 3.5 亿元，引进 120 家大型客商和 600 家电商，导入创业人才 3 万人左右。

# Fuyang Silicon Valley Town

---

Silicon Valley，in the northern part of the state of California，U.S.，is now the home to many of the world's largest high-tech corporations，including the headquarters of 39 businesses in the 10000 companies issued by *Fortune*，and thousands of startup companies. Today，in Fuyang district of Hangzhou city，there also comes a place called "Silicon Valley Town," a town full of innovative vitality.

Fuyang Silicon Valley Town covers about 3.1 square kilometers. Recently it successfully introduced six major industrial projects：Tian'an • Fuchun Silicon Valley，Insigma，China's Zhigu Park，Silver Lake Innovation Center，Sheng Hong Industrial Design Park，and Xiongmai Information Group，with a total investment of more than seven billion yuan. Now，it vigorously fosters more than 40 growth-oriented enterprises such as Tongxing Technology，E-Lake Network，and Byte Information.

Fuyang Silicon Valley is also called "Tian'an • Fuchun Silicon Valley." In fact，it is only part of the "Silicon Valley Town，" but it is the core and engine of the "Silicon Valley Town." In 2013，the Fuchun Silicon Valley got off the ground in Silver Lake Science and Technology City，with a total investment of three billion to be completed in 2017. Such an area， which has not yet been built, has attracted 40 intelligent enterprises that decided to settle there. Walking in Fuchun Silicon Valley makes people feel as if they were in United States Silicon Valley's casual and relaxed environment which offers a variety of technology products that visitors give a "thumbs-up" to.

What's more, it provides good services. When other enterprises are busy with a variety of formalities, the companies in Fuchun Silicon Valley have been enjoying the service of "Bag Check." The responsible official there says that they start to provide advice and services to enterprises before they enter. After the enterprises decides to settle there, the town offers "one-stop" services to them. At the same time, in cooperation with the Hangzhou Municipal Commission of Economy and Information Technology, the "Fuyang SME Service Center" moves into Silicon Valley, which was very convenient for the future settled enterprises.

In addition, the Fuchun Silicon Valley implements the "Business Plan" to help enterprises. First, through the construction and operation of the "incubator," it assists them in the birth of a number of small and medium intelligent enterprises. Then through the "accelerator" it promotes the rapid growth and development of these enterprises. At last, by technology, network and data, it supports these enterprises to expand the scale and complete transformation and upgrading. For example, the town builds a research support center, financial service centers, and other platforms to help enterprises grow efficiently. Their objectives are clearly seen on a wall of the Fuchun Silicon Valley, which states the town will introduce 500 enterprises by

2017 and attract 20000 high-end talents. By year-end, the annual output value will reach 300 billion yuan, with annual profits and taxes hitting the 1. 5 billion mark.

The Silicon Valley Town is not only an industrial town, but also a tourism town. Fuyang has ecological environment with picturesque scenery in beautiful mountains and clear rivers. Tianmu Mountain stretches through the northwest, Xianxia Ridge winds its way southeast, and Fuchun River passes through the west into the east.

over 600 years ago, Huang Gongwang, the Yuan Dynasty painter, told the world that Fuyang was a livable, appropriate place through his greatest work "Dwelling in the Fuchun Mountains." Today Fuyang shows a modern picture of natural scenery and industrial vitality. Chen Hailong, Deputy Director of Fuyang Development and Reform Bureau, said, "East China's largest wildlife park, opposite of Silicon Valley Town, hosts more than 2 million visitors each year. There are also leisure and sightseeing places such as Wuchao Mountain, Huang

Gongwang National Forest Park, and International Golf Course as well. The outdoor camping base of the Yangtze River Delta is an ecological resource that's very rich."

"To optimize the environment, and to keep talents maintained, Silicon Valley Town vigorously supports the implementation of life and convenience," Wang Wu said. Silver Lake Experimental School is expected to open next year with the investment of 960 million yuan. In addition, the technologically-talented apartment complex is under construction with large and medium-sized medical institutions and community hospitals. Additional bus lines have opened to solve the traffic problems of employees in the small town of Silicon Valley. In the meantime, the town will also create "15-minute life circles," improved coffee bars, a multi-function conference center, convenience stores, and introduce the Fuyang Agricultural Bank, Huachen Supermarket, cafeteria and other supporting projects that create a wonderful town atmosphere.

According to the plan, after 3 to 5 years of construction, the Silicon Valley Town will become a new community with a set of high-tech industries, deep cultural heritage, and beautiful environment. The Silicon Valley Town is the first project of Fuyang, and will further gather scientific research institutions and economic enterprises, to actively develop information technology, and industrial design, which will play the main position in the Fuyang's development of information economy. By then, the Silicon Valley Town will become a demonstration area with the masses starting their businesses and people beginning to innovate.

# 富阳硅谷小镇

硅谷,位于美国加利福尼亚北部,是许多高科技公司所在地,包括《财富》公布的 1000 强企业中的 39 家的总部,以及数千家创业公司。今天,在富阳,同样也有一个充满创新活力的硅谷小镇,被称为"富阳硅谷小镇"。

富阳硅谷小镇规划面积为 3.1 平方千米,核心区面积为 1 平方千米。目前已成功引进六个重大产业项目:天安·富春硅谷、浙大网新、中国智谷富阳园区、银湖创新中心、颐高圣泓工业设计园、雄迈信息集团总部基地,总投资超过 70 亿元。现在还正在大力培育 40 多家成长型企业,如同兴科技、易莱克网络、字节信息等。

富阳硅谷小镇也会被人们称为"天安·富春硅谷"。事实上,富春硅谷仅仅是整个"硅谷小镇"里的一部分,不过它是核心部分,是整个"硅谷小镇"的核心引擎。2013 年,富春硅谷落地银湖科技城,总投资 30 亿,计划 2017 年年底完成。这样一个智慧园区尚未建成前,就吸引了 40 家智慧型企业决定入驻。走在富春硅谷园区,人们仿佛置身于美国的"硅谷",休闲轻松的办公环境,各种高科技产品,让参观者连连点赞。

更重要的是,小镇为入驻企业提供了良好的服务。当其他企业还在忙于各种手续时,富春硅谷的企业已经在享受着"拎包入住"式服务了。富春硅谷的负责人介绍说,企业没入驻前,他们已经开始向企业提供咨询和服务;企业决定落户后,小镇便为他们提供"一站式"服务。同时,富春硅谷与杭州市经济和信息化委员会的中小企业服务中心合作,将"中小企业服务富阳中心"放到了富春硅谷,这将为未来入驻企业提供非常方便的服务。

此外,富春硅谷对企业实施"陪商计划"。首先,通过"孵化器"的建设和运营,诞生一批智慧型的中小企业,然后通过"加速器"促进这些企业的快速成长和发展。最后利用技术、网络和大数据,支持这些企业扩大规模,完成转型升级,通过建立科研支持中心、金融服务等平台,帮助企业高效成长。富春硅谷园区建成后将引进企业 500 家,吸引高端人才 20000 名,预计年产值达到 300 亿元,年创利税 15 亿元。

富阳硅谷小镇既是一个工业小镇,又是一个旅游小镇。富阳山川秀美,河流清澈,生态环境优美。富春江西入东出,穿境而过。600 多年前,元代大画家黄公望就通过《富春山居图》告诉世人,富阳是一个宜居、宜业、宜游的好地方。时过境迁,今天的富阳展现了一幅集自然风光和产业活力的现代化的富春山居图。在富阳硅谷小镇区内,富春硅谷对面就是华东地区最大的野生动物园,年游客量达 200 余万人次。附近还有午潮山、黄公望两家国家森林公园和国际高尔夫球场,以及长三角(新沙岛)户外露营基地等休闲观光资源,生态资源非常丰富。

为优化环境,留住人才,富阳硅谷小镇在区域内将建设银湖实验学校、科技人才公寓、大型医疗机构和社区医院等配套设施,另外,增设公交线路解决硅谷小镇职工交通问题。同时,小镇还将打造"15 分钟生活圈",完善咖啡酒吧、多功能会议中心、便利店等小商铺,引进富阳农业银行、华辰超市、职工餐厅等项目,打造美好的生活氛围。

按照规划,通过 3 至 5 年的建设,富阳硅谷小镇将成为一个具有高科技产业、文化底蕴深厚、旅游多元化及环境优美的新型社区。硅谷小镇,作为杭州主城区进入富阳的第一站,将进一步聚集科研机构和智慧经济企业,积极发展信息技术,工业设计等产业,成为富阳发展信息经济的主阵地。届时,富阳硅谷小镇将成为"大众创业、万众创新"的示范区,杭州西部信息经济发展的集聚区。

# Tonglu Health Town

Tonglu, an ancient administrative district, was named for an old man named Tong Jun, who built houses (Lu) in a mountain that was later named after him, made medicine with herbs and cured sickness to save patients. According to the legend, Tongjun, as an ancient pharmacist and minister of Yellow Emperor, was good at herbal medicine. Therefore Tonglu, in the minds of people, has become a veritable "Holy Land of Chinese Medicine."

It is precisely because of this unique cultural foundation of Chinese medicine that since 2013, the Tonglu county government has actively seized the development opportunities of health services industries, and built the Health City of Mount Fuchun next to the Daqishan Mountain National Forest Park. After more than a year's development, the Health City of Mount Fuchun has begun to take shape, which lays a solid foundation for the future construction of the Tonglu Health Town.

Choosing the sites for the Health City of Mount Fuchun and the future Health Town was also a painstaking effort. Today the Health Town, with its back against the Daqishan mountain National Forest Park, is surrounded by mountains and faces the Fuchun River, which is like a paradise. The whole area has obvious environmental advantages: the forest coverage rate is more than 80%; air quality meets or surpasses the secondary standard; the PM 2. 5 annual average value is below 35 and the air is rich in negative oxygen ions, that is, 2578 per cubic centimeter, far exceeding the national six-level standard. In addition, the average annual temperature is 15 degrees in the region, with 26 degrees in the summer, which is equal to the summer resort Lushan National Park. Also, because of the Fuchun River, the Health Town's water standard is reaching 100% excellence. What's more, the Health Town retains the ancient ecological villages, and the ecological environment of less population density, all of which showing the Health Town is worth expecting.

In the future there will also appear several major functional areas. First, the Ruijin-Mount Fuchun Health Care Base with a total investment of 1 billion yuan covers an approximate 200000 square meters, which will be built as a health complex with high-end medical and third-party testing center, physical examination center, nursing center, and Chinese herbal medicine cultivation center. At present, the company has completed the formation and pre-program planning. Second, the Wanxiang aged-care and tourism complex, which plans to use about 333 thousand square meters land, is a program with a total investment of about 1.5 billion that is mainly from the Wanxiang Group. It will include a "Happy and Healthy Center," a Wuli Gallery, two "Lehuo" parks, five Xinsu places and so on. Thee construction of the complex began in November. Third, the "Lujing" project by the Greatstar Group which has invested 300 million yuan in total and 27000 square meters of land, plans to use gentle slopes between two natural valleys to build a high-end personalized landscape resort health hotel.

Building the Tonglu Health Town has been delightful, while the town's future health industries and functions are worth looking forward to. An ecological and modern health base is emerging. In the next three years, the accumulated investment will reach 6.1 billion yuan in fixed assets, with 5 billion yuan of total output, 680 million yuan as the total tax revenue, and the number of tourists reaching 1.8 million.

# 桐庐健康小镇

桐庐，古老的行政区名，得名于一个名叫桐君的老人，他在桐君山下结庐采药，用药草治病救人。根据传说，桐君老人是上古时的药学家，黄帝之臣，以擅长本草著称。因此，桐庐在人们的心中，已成为名副其实的"中医药鼻祖圣地"。

由于这一独特的中医文化基础，桐庐县政府自 2013 年起，就积极抓住健康服务业这一朝阳产业的发展机遇，在大奇山国家森林公园旁建立了富春山健康城。经过一年多的发展，富春山健康城已经初具雏形，为桐庐健康小镇未来的建设奠定了坚实的基础。

在富春山健康城及桐庐健康小镇的选址方面，政府也是费尽了心思。今天的桐庐健康小镇背靠大奇山国家森林公园，三面环山，一面临着富春江，宛如世外仙境。整个区域环境优势明显：森林覆盖率超过 80%，每年有340 天的空气质量达到或超过二级标准天数，PM2.5 年平均值低于 35，空气中富含丰富的负氧离子，每立方厘米达到 2578 个，远远超过国家六级标准。此外，该地区的年平均气温为 15 摄氏度，酷暑天也在 26 度左右，比起避暑胜地庐山也不遑多让。而且，小镇的水资源达标率达到 100%，镇区域内还保留着古老的生态村、人口密度较低的生态环境。这一切都说明了桐庐健康小镇值得期待。

未来的桐庐健康小镇还会出现几个主要功能区，重点打造三个项目：一是瑞金·富春山居医疗养生基地，总投资 10 亿元，占地 20 万平方米，将建设为集高端医疗和第三方检测中心、体检中心、护理中心、中草药种植等为一体的养生综合体;二是万向养生养老旅游综合体,规划占地约33.3万平方米,总投资约15亿元,由万向集团投资,建设成集乐养中心、五里画廊、乐活两园、心宿五村等为一体的养生养老旅游综合体;三是巨星控股集团"庐境"项目,总投资3亿元,总规划用地2.7万平方米,计划利用两个自然山谷间的缓坡平地建设一个以自然生态、幽静私密为特色的高档个性化景观度假养生酒店。

桐庐健康小镇的建设现状已经让人欣喜,而未来健康小镇的规模、产业、功能将更加值得期待,一个兼具原生态和现代化的养生基地已初现端倪。在未来三年内,小镇将实现固定资产累计投入达61亿元,累计产出50亿元,累计税收6.8亿元,旅游人数达到180万人次。

# Lin'an Cloud Manufacturing Town

"Trees grow by the water, boats sail on the lake in the forests, birds sing on the branches, and people walk along the lake," this beautiful scenery can be viewed from the Qingshan Lake, Lin'an. Located near the Qingshan Lake, Lin'an, the Cloud Manufacturing Town enjoys this natural treasure.

People may be wondering what kind of "small town" this is? Simply put, it is an innovative platform. Known as the platform for intelligent equipment manufacturing, it represents a new generation of information technology that realizes product development and product sales, and provides standard, shareable manufacturing services.

The total planning area of the Cloud Manufacturing Town is 3. 17 square kilometers. It includes a development axis, a passage, and two areas. the "development axis" is the innovative economic axis of the Park Road; The "passage" refers to a landscape corridor along Shaoxi green waterway, and the "two areas" include business and service platforms and an upgrading area of intelligent equipment. Generally speaking, the Cloud Manufacturing Town has three main characteristics as follows.

First, the town incorporates manufacturing into the tide of "Internet Plus." At present, information technology is highly fused into manufacturing to speed up the transformation of economic development, to promote science and technological revolution, and to make industrial revolution become the top priority of economic construction. How manufacturing can be incorporated into the tide of "Internet Plus" and keep up with the pace of industrial 4. 0 has become the major problem faced by the manufacturing industry.

Lin'an is among the first national ecological cities and China's most excellent tourist resorts. With its good ecological resources, Lin'an also hopes to develop its economy. In 2009, the Zhejiang provincial government decided to build a new town of science and technology. Finally, it chose its location in the Qingshan Lake, Lin'an. Through five years of construction, with more than 30 billion industrial sales, 46 scientific research institutes settled in the town with its name "Cloud Manufacturing Town." Today, the scientific research institutes have combined their unique talents, information, technology, and scientific research equipment resources. "These 46 scientific research institutes are all committed to intelligent manufacturing. We are professionals in industrial 4.0. This is the right place for both of us!" General Manager Zhou Says, who is from Zhejiang Indusfo Software Technology Co., Ltd.

Second, the town has attracted a group of makers sticking to industrial intelligent reform. In the buildings of the Cloud Manufacturing Town, there is a group of young men from Zhejiang University who founded Hangzhou Leaper Technology Co., Ltd. They are dedicated to improving the performance of the "Depth Camera." Today's camera can only produce two-dimensional pictures, but Depth Camera they are researching can precisely calculate distance of imaging objects and can even be used for indoor and outdoor imaging which may reach several kilometers away. These techniques can be applied into automatic driving, mechanical arm manufacturing, intelligent security, and other fields. From defect detection to imaging search, and then to depth camera, it only takes three years for Leaper Technology, which increases and writes legend for Leaper.

Settled in the Cloud Manufacturing Town, 26 small and medium-sized science and technology companies have the same ambition as the Leaper Group. These young men are dedicated to intelligent industrial innovation, giving the Cloud Manufacturing Town infinite growth power.

Third, 46 scientific research institutions gives the town a strong scientific research support. One official from Hangzhou Qingshan

Lake High-tech Industrial Park Management Committee says, there will be 46 research institutes located here from the University of Hong Kong, Changchun Institute of Applied Chemistry Chinese Academy of Sciences, China University of Geosciences, Xi'an Jiaotong University and so on, and the town will be the largest gathering of research institutions in Zhejiang Province. At the same time they will bring more than 2000 high-level talents, among which are 15 academicians, 32 persons from "National Thousand" and "Provincial Thousand" talents. More than 110 manufacturing enterprises and 38 high-tech enterprises such as Hangcha Group Co., Ltd., Xizi UHC Co., Ltd., and Wanma Group Co., Ltd. will settle in the town, and they will provide strong manufacturing support for the Cloud Manufacturing Town.

In order to develop more quickly, the Cloud Manufacturing Town unites research institutes and enterprises to promote building, professional testing centers, service platforms, and high quality R&D resources, to insure that they can achieve the goal of mutual development and promote collaborative innovation. At the same time, the Cloud Manufacturing Town establishes an open innovative service platform, through which enterprises can transfer technology, provide service solutions to effectively promote the efficient use of production resources for the realization of collaborative, green, intelligent production.

During the next three years, the Cloud Manufacturing Town will develop into a town with financial cloud manufacturing services, technology, research and development, business innovation, cultural tourism and other functions. By 2017, the town is expected to achieve a total output value of 23. 95 billion yuan, a total tax revenue of 1. 28 billion yuan, and to attract more than 400000 tourists. This constitutes Lin'an's practice of the "Green Mountains and Clear Rivers are Treasure" theory.

# 临安云制造小镇

"树在水中长，船在林间行，鸟在枝上鸣，人在画中行"，青山湖的秀美风景可见一斑，位于临安青山湖的云制造小镇自然享受了这一自然瑰宝。

临安云制造小镇到底是什么样的"小镇"呢？简而言之，它是一个创新平台，利用新一代信息技术的智能设备制造，实现产品开发销售，提供标准化、可共享的制造服务。云制造小镇规划面积的 3.17 平方千米，总体布局包括"一轴一脉两区"。"一轴"即大园路创新发展轴，"一脉"即苕溪绿色水脉景观走廊，"两区"即核心区众创空间和智能装备提升区。总体而言，临安云制造小镇具有以下特色。

首先，小镇将制造业融入"互联网＋"的大潮。当前，信息技术高度融入制造业，加快经济发展转型，促进科技革命和产业革命成为经济建设的重中之重。如何将制造业的转型升级融入"互联网＋"的潮流，跟上工业 4.0 的步伐，已成为成为当下制造业着力思考的问题。

临安是首批全国生态建设示范市和中国优秀旅游胜地之一，具有良好的生态资源，同样萌发着现代经济的新芽。2009 年，浙江省委省政府决定打造一个科技新城，最终选择了临安市青山湖。经过五年的建设，已有 46 家科研院所入驻，拥有 300 多亿的工业销售额。现在，这些科研机构形成了独特的人才、信息、技术、科研设备资源。"46 家科研机构都致力于智能制造，而我们专业做工业 4.0 方面的工作，落户这里，我们选对了地方。"浙江恩大施福软件科技有限公司负责人说，他们是入驻小镇的企业之一，最看重的就是小镇的制造业氛围。

其次,小镇有一批执着于工业智能化改造的青年创客。在云制造小镇的大楼中,一批来自浙江大学的年轻人成立了杭州利珀科技有限公司,他们正在研发性能领先的深度相机。目前的相机只能拍出二维平面,但他们正在研究的深度相机可以精确计算成像物体的间距,甚至可以用于室内外成像,距离可能达到几千米远。这些技术可应用于自动驾驶、机械臂制造、智能安防等领域。从产品缺陷检测到图像搜索技术,然后到深度相机,利珀科技有限公司的建立只用了三年,其敢想敢做的利珀团队书写着利珀的传奇。落户云制造小镇的26家中小科技公司,都有着与利珀科技有限公司同样的雄心。这些年轻人致力于工业智能化改造,赋予了云制造小镇无限的生长力。

最后,46家科研院所的落户为小镇提供了强大的科研支撑。在科研方面,临安云制造小镇将有香港大学浙江研究院、中国科学院长春应用化学研究所、中国地质大学浙江研究院、西安交通大学浙江研究院等46家科研院所落户,这里将是浙江省最大的研究机构聚集地。同时他们将带来2000多名高级人才,其中包括15名院士、32名"国千"和"省千"人才。在产业入驻方面,将有如杭叉集团有限公司、西子联合、万马股份等110多家制造企业和38家高新技术企业在这里集群发展。这些大院名所,将为云制造小镇提供强大的科研力量。

为了加快小镇的发展,云制造小镇整合科研院所和企业的研发资源,促进共建专业检测中心、服务平台,实现高质量的研发资源,使他们实现相互发展,助推院所和企业协同创新。同时,云制造小镇建立了开放式创新服务平台,企业可以通过平台转让技术,提供服务解决方案,有效促进生产资源的高效利用,为实现协同、敏捷、绿色、智能化生产提供创新服务。

未来三年,云制造小镇将发展成为融云制造服务、科技研发、创业创新、文化展示、旅游休闲、生活居住、社区服务等功能为一体的特色小镇。

到 2017 年年底，该镇预计实现总产值 239.95 亿元，税收总额 12.8 亿元，吸引游客 40 多万人次，这是临安对"绿水青山就是金山银山"理论的又一实践。

# Ningbo

宁 波

# Jiangbei Power Town

Located in the Ningbo High-Tech Industrial Park in Cicheng Town, the Jiangbei Power Town leans on the Zhejiang Province's "Thousand Talents Program" Industrial Park in the west, against an ecological touring road in the north, Ningbo E-commerce Industrial Park in the east, and the Ci River, part of Beijing-Hangzhou Grand Canal, in the south, showing the town has obvious advantages in its geographical location.

The total planning area for the Jiangbei Power Town was about 3. 3 square kilometers with a core area of 1. 5 square kilometers. In the past, Cicheng Town was mainly composed of traditional industries in the industrial structure, which had a lack of characteristic industrial positioning. In 2015, the idea of the characteristic town construction provided a viable road for the town's industrial innovation and industry upgrades in the future. According to Development and Reform Bureau Jiangbei District in Ningbo, the Power Town was mainly invested by the China State Shipbuilding Corporation and Liandong investment Co. , Ltd. With the Ningbo's Hi-Tech Industrial Park as the development platform, its mode of operation was led by the business-oriented projects to attract foreign businesses and investment.

On the basis of the cooperation agreement, the China Shipbuilding Group will be building "one garden and one institute" in the town, which will become a new engine in the rapid operation of the modern industrial system. "one garden" will be the production base for power integrated equipment such as a shield production base and a high-power diesel engine research & production center; "one institute" refers to an equipment power research institute that focuses on marine equipment power industry research, design and its industrialization, which will gradually build into a national research institution to promote marine equipment, power technology progress and development. Currently there have been 11 enterprises in the park including superior companies such as Samsung Electronics, Liandong U Valley, Exciton Technology Co., Ltd., and Ningbo Ruiyuan Biotechnology Co., Ltd. At the same time, the local government is also actively promoting subsidiary industries like new materials, electro mechanics, information and control which can lead to industrial integration. In addition, Cicheng will strengthen cooperation with the Central SOEs and large enterprises to strengthen industrial and technology investment, attracting a number of high-end projects and excellent enterprises in order to achieve a great situation.

In order to promote the sustainable development, the Power Town, on one hand, is actively introducing high-end talents. At the present, the town has four people from the national "Thousands of People Plan," one from the provincial "Thousand Plan." and more than 65 people who hold Masters Degrees. It also possesses more than 60 kinds of patents, including 13 invention authorizations. Considering the development needs of the industry, the Power Town will recruit, in a timely manner, academicians, well-known experts, Doctors and other high-end talents who support industrial development.

On the other hand, the Power Town will pay more attention to the culture and ecology strategy. In history, Cicheng has been known as the town full of Jinshi (successful candidate in the highest imperid examinations). From the Tang and Song to the Ming and Qing Dynasties, there have been a total of 519 Jinshi in the highest imperial examinations. In modern times, there has been a lot of cultural celebrities, such as the Peking Opera Master Zhou Xinfang, the founder of modern Chinese genetics Tan Jiazhen, and the famous writer and folk cultural heritage protector Feng Jicai. Until now, Cicheng's scholarly fame could be found. Cicheng ancient county has also developed seven tourist attractions such as the Confucius Temple,

the Ancient County Government, the School Scholar Museum, and the Feng Yu house, which completes the public landscape transformation of 330000 square meters, and explores the tertiary industry for the coordination of cultural and creative exhibition with the ancient city.

The introduction of the "Projects, Talents and Ecology" has been the driving force for the Power town's take-off. At the end of 2015, Cicheng's total GDP exceeded 6 billion yuan, ranking the first with a growth rate of 12% among the city's eight satellite towns. In January, 2016, the fiscal revenue of the town reached 170 million yuan, increasing by 63% when compared to that of the past year. The Power Town is building a higher starting point in the economic development.

# 江北动力小镇

江北区动力小镇位于宁波（江北）高新技术产业园区，西靠浙江省"千人计划"产业园，北拥国家级北山生态游步道，东接宁波电商产业园，南临京杭大运河的组成部分——慈江。小镇总规划面积约 3.3 平方千米，核心区约 1.5 平方千米。

江北动力小镇，位于慈城镇，该原有产业结构以传统产业为主，缺乏特色产业定位，浙江省提出的特色小镇建设思路，给小镇在产业集聚、产业创新和产业升级等方面提供了一条可行道路。据宁波市江北区发展和改革局介绍，江北动力小镇由中国船舶工业集团公司（央企，以下简称"中船集团"）、联东投资集团有限公司（民企）作为投资主体，以宁波（江北）高新技术产业园为发展平台，其运作模式是由企业主导项目建设，以新项目为主开展招商引资。

根据双方合作协议，中船集团将在小镇建设"一园一院"。"一园一院"将成为动力小镇在现代产业体系飞速运转中的新引擎。"一园"是中船（宁波）装备产业园，将主要建设和发展中船动力与宁波中策合作项目、盾构生产基地、齿轮箱和螺旋桨等动力集成装置生产基地、大功率柴油机研发及生产基地；"一院"是指装备动力研究院，它主要聚焦海洋装备动力产业研究设计及其产业化，将逐步建设成国家级研究机构，推动海洋装备动力技术进步和发展。目前在园企业集聚了三星、联东 U 谷、激智科技、瑞源生物等优势企业，"智能电表、膜材料、科技型小微企业"三大产业集群发展态势进一步形成。同时，当地政府还积极推动新材料、机电与电子、信息与控制、新能源等上下游配套产业的发展，促进要素集聚和产业融合发展，打造国内一流的高端海洋工程动力装备制造业。此外，小镇还将加强与央企、大企业的合作，强化产业招商、科技招商、以商引商，招引一批高端高效、高附加值、高产出率的优质项目和优秀企业，并加快对科技型中小企业的引进、培育和发展，从而实现"引进一个，带动一批，影响一片"的良好态势。

为了推动项目持续发展，动力小镇还积极引进高端人才，小镇目前有国家"千人计划"4人，省级"千人计划"1人，硕士及硕士以上人才65人，获得各类专利60余项，其中发明授权13项。

文化是特色小镇的灵魂，是特色小镇持续发展的生命张力。江北动力小镇在历史上曾是远近闻名的"进士之乡"，从唐宋至明清，共出了519名进士。到近现代，这里也涌现过很多文化名人，比如京剧大师周信芳、中国现代遗传学奠基人谈家桢，以及著名作家、民间文化遗产保护者冯骥才等。直到今天，小镇内的书香古风依旧可觅。目前，小镇已开发了孔庙、古县衙、校士馆、冯俞宅等7个旅游景点，完成公共景观改造33万平方米，并探索引入了文化创意展示等与古城相协调的第三产业。下一步，当地政府将把动力小镇建设与"文化立镇""生态美镇"战略结合起来，着力发挥好文化底色和生态底色两大"镇城之宝"，建设更加宜业、宜居的动力小镇。

项目落地、人才的引进、生态观念的重视为动力小镇插上了腾飞的翅膀。2015年小镇生产总量突破60亿元，以12%位居全市卫星城生产总量增幅榜首，成为全市八个卫星城试点镇唯一保持两位数增长的卫星镇。江北动力小镇正在着力构筑发展跨越的高起点……

# Meishan Marine Financial Town

In 2011, the State Council officially approved the Programme of Zhejiang Demonstrative Marine Economic Development Areas, so the construction of the Zhejiang Marine Economic Zone rose to a national strategy. The Ningbo-Zhoushan Port Area and its support cities become the core area. However, the development of the marine economy was inseparable from finance in the modern market economy. If the marine economy is like a growing youth, finance is his blood to sustain his vitality. In modern history, Ningbo has been a well-developed financial center in the southeast coastal region, which cannot be absent in the historical opportunity of the marine economy. Hence, the Meishan Marine Financial Town was born.

The Meishan Marine Financial Town is located in the central area of Meishan Bay and includes two sides of the Meishan Bridge. Its total area is about 3.5 square kilometers, with about 1 square kilometer as the core area. The town is composed of "two cores and two gardens." Specifically, the "two cores" are divided by Meishan Avenue. In the North there is the Marine Financial Research and Development Training Experimental Zone, which is a high-end private-sharing interactive area with a Financial Information Service Platform Area to develop the headquarters' economy, and financial data and public information service economy. In the South, locate the Marine Financial Innovation Base, Marine Financial High-end Conference Area and the Coastal Financial Creative Display Area, to promote the marine financial scientific research, conference-orientated economy, financial knowledge and new product exhibition. The "two gardens" are bound by Meishan Bay, with a high-end Physical Therapy Treatment Zone on the eastern side, mainly for physical examination and customized physical therapy. In the western side is the Health-Care Culture Resort for leisure resort projects.

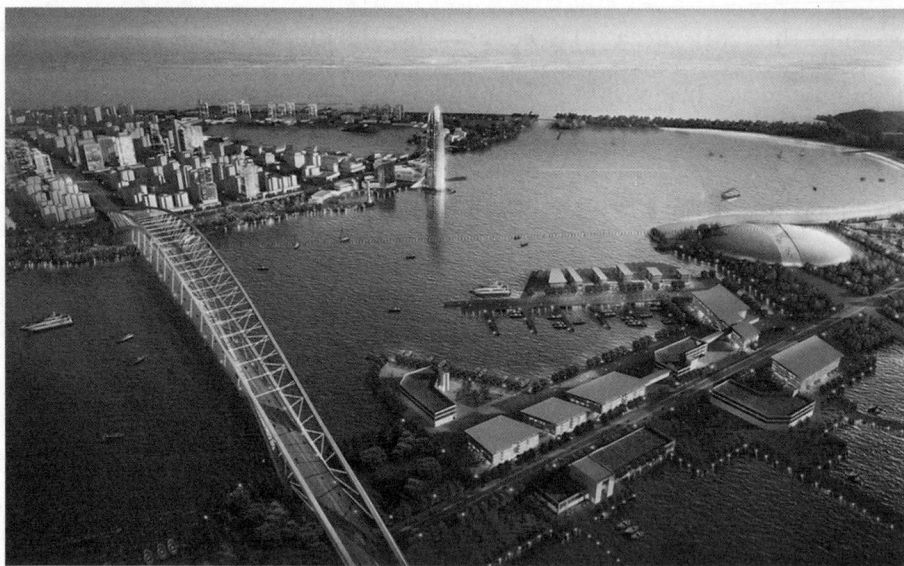

With the support of the national financial strategy, in recent years Meishan has developed quickly with its own advantages. Until now, it has introduced more than 1500 financial enterprises. Its industrial density is the highest in the province. There also exists a trend that similar financial enterprises are gradually expanding. For example, the Ningbo Qiushi Investment and Management Co., Ltd., after its capital increase of 10 billion yuan, owned the registered capital of more than 16 billion yuan, becoming the region's largest investment enterprises. At the same time, the town attracted a large number of finance leasing companies to come, such as the Uni-Power Group, Ningbo Donghai Leasing Co., Ltd., and Tianxin Investment. Up to now, Meishan has accumulated 33 financial leasing enterprises, with the cumulative leased assets of more than 4 billion yuan. Although the development time is short, financial leasing companies are closely connected with local industries, covering new energy, equipment manufacturing and public transportation, which has aroused special attention from the Meishan Marine Financial Town.

From the initial capital and business drawing to the present policy of introducing only the excellent enterprises, Meishan is confident enough to build a billion-level "Wealth Management Island" and create a new financial future.

# 梅山海洋金融小镇

2011 年,国务院正式批复《浙江海洋经济发展示范区规划》,浙江海洋经济区建设上升为国家战略。宁波—舟山港海域及其依托城市成为该发展示范区的核心区。海洋经济的概念与规划提出来之后,一个想象空间巨大、全新的经济领域呈现在宁波的面前。发展海洋经济,在现代市场经济条件下,是离不开金融的,如果说海洋经济是日益茁壮成长的青年,那海洋金融就是维持其朝气与活力的血脉。在我国近代史上,宁波的金融就非常发达,一度是东南沿海的金融中心。拥有如此优势,当然不能在海洋经济的历史机遇中缺席。于是,梅山海洋金融小镇破冰而来。

梅山海洋金融小镇位于梅山湾中部、梅山大桥两岸区域,总面积约 3.5 平方千米,核心区约 1 平方千米。小镇规划结构为"双核双园"。具体而言:"双核",即以梅山大道为分界线,北区为海洋金融研发培训实验区、类金融机构高端私享互动区和金融信息服务公共平台区,主要发展总部经济、金融大数据和公共信息服务经济等;南区为海洋金融创新基地、海洋金融高端会务区和滨海金融创意展示区,主要发展海洋金融产业科研经济、会务经济、金融知识科普展和新产品展示经济。"双园",以梅山湾为界,东侧为高端体检理疗区,主要为金融高端人士提供体检和定制理疗服务;西侧为养生文化度假区,主要为金融圈人士提供休闲养生度假项目。

在国家金融创新战略的推进下,梅山近几年结合自身优势,发展迅速。截至 2015 年 5 月,全区已累计引进 1500 多家类金融企业,这样的密度在省内是最高的。类金融企业单体投资规模呈逐步扩大趋势,如宁波秋实投资管理合伙企业(有限合伙)增资 100 亿元后,注册资本超过 160 亿元,成为目前区内注册规模最大的投资类企业之一。小镇同样吸引了东海融资、天信、中新力合等一大批融资租赁公司前来注册,累计已设融资租赁企业 33 家,租赁资产余额逾 40 亿元。融资租赁虽在宁波发展时间较短,但与地方产业结合紧密,业务涵盖新能源、装备制造和公共交通等领域,因而受到了海洋金融小镇的特别关注。

从最初的招商,到现在的选商,梅山已经用自信和底气构筑起了千亿级"财富管理岛"的品牌高度,创享金融未来。

# Fenghua Coastal Health Town

The Fenghua Coastal Health Town, located in the north part of Xiangshan Port, is under the jurisdiction of the national key town Qiucun Town. Qiucun Town is a typical coastal eco-town with a long history and rich culture. The town is surrounded by sea and islands, and features forests and wetlands, with the largest island in Xiangshan Port, Gangpanshan Island. The island has three major ecological natural resources: the Wild Beach Hibiscus Protection Area, a Rare Bird Protection Area in Nansha Mountain Island and an Ecological Protection Area in the Hengjiang wetland. In recent years, the Qiucun Town, with a resource endowment from a development foundation, made full use of the ecological resources to actively promote coastal tourism, so that the coastal town can become more liveable.

In 2016, to speed up the construction of Fenghua Coastal Health Town, Fenghua Coastal Health Town adjusted the Qiucun Town's planning to gradually strengthen the rural infrastructure, the environmental remediation, and the village's transformation. First, it plans to create a tourism atmosphere of Huangxian Village, by improving Huangxian Forest Park's 4A National Scenic Area, and by speeding up the construction of the Theme Alley. Second, it will strive to re-build Matou Village, a village with the characteristics of the Republic of China. Matou Village has more than 1100 years of history. It still retains a large number of ancient buildings and other historical sites from the Ming and Qing Dynasties, and the Republic of China. It was also known as the "Professor Village." Since the Republic of China, Matou Village has produced dozens of scholars, professors, and experts. Also in order to retain these historic sites, the town plans to invest more than 60 million yuan, to repair part of the old houses and restore the two cobblestone roads. Thirdly, the Fenghua Coastal Health Town has pushed the "Shiyan Village Coastal Project" again. Shiyan village, for the purpose of "the whole village transformation," highlights the tourism development as part of the implementation of the "Seaside Reed Fishing Base" and the "Gang Panshan Island Development" projects. In addition, the town has actively explored eco-tourism potentials, and developed the Shiyan Xiaoxi Mountain, and other hiking trails.

What's more, to give full play to the advantages of human resources and build cultural plates of historical ancient village, the Fenghua Coastal Health Town will add the "Health and Entertainment" idea into the construction. Its core industries include a Spa and meditation center, a care service area, the Sea Silk Road Paradise, a duty-free shopping center, the Ocean Resort Hotel and a large sea-side entertainment center. These projects are the highlights of the sports industry and are the core of the plan.

# 奉化滨海养生小镇

奉化滨海养生小镇位于象山港北侧，属省级中心镇、全国重点乡镇裘村镇辖区。裘村镇历史悠久，人文荟萃，是典型的"滨海生态镇"。镇内海洋、岛屿、森林、湿地资源丰富，拥有象山港内最大的岛屿——缸爿山岛，而缸爿山岛野生海滨木槿保护区、南沙山岛珍稀鸟类保护区、横江湿地生态保护区是全镇三大特色生态自然资源，并被列入宁波市级生态保护区。近年来，裘村镇立足资源禀赋和发展基础，充分挖掘和利用生态资源，积极推动滨海旅游精品线建设，让滨海小镇更加宜居。

2016年，为加快建设奉化滨海养生小镇的步伐，裘村镇因村制宜调整村庄规划，配套细化建设方案，加强农村基础设施建设、环境整治和旧村改造，通过"示范点、精品线"的重点突破，全面实施基础设施建设。一是营造黄贤村旅游氛围。以"村景合一"建设为愿景，完善黄贤森林公园景区国家4A级景区旅游功能，加快村庄环境整治、建设主题弄堂、发展民宿经济。二是打造民国特色的"水墨马头"。马头村迄今已有1100多年的历史，沉淀着厚重的人文历史。村内的民清旧居基本处于原生状态，现仍保留着一大批明清、民国时期的古建筑群和古樟、古井等古迹遗存。自民国时期以来，马头村就出了几十名学者教授、专家博士，曾被誉为"教授村"。三是重推石沿滨海项目。石沿村以"整村改造"为基础，开发旅游亮点，实施海滨芦苇垂钓基地、缸爿山海岛开发等项目。另外，裘村镇积极挖掘生态旅游的特色和亮点，开发甲岙菩提、马头鸡鹑、石沿小西天等登山步道。

　　发挥人文资源优势,打造历史古村文化板块,奉化滨海养生小镇还将以康体养生产业为核心,建设温泉疗养中心、健康养生养老综合服务区、海上丝绸之路乐园一期、免税购物中心、海洋之心度假酒店和大型海秀演艺中心等核心项目。

**Wenzhou**

温 州

# Ouhai Fashion Manufacturing Town

Wenzhou, as the pioneer of China's private economy development, always stands out in the manufacturing frontline in China's reform and opening up, and has been known at home and abroad. In recent years, in order to adapt to the "new normal" economy, the Wenzhou municipal government has put forward the strategy of constructing a "Fashion Town," to promote the industrial transformation from "Made in Wenzhou" to "Made with Wisdom" and thus upgrade from traditional industries to the fashion industry. The Wenzhou Ouhai District has firmly grasped the opportunity. According to the existing industrial infrastructure and industrial development orientation of Wenzhou City and Ouhai District, it has put forward the idea of building an "Ouhai Fashion Manufacturing Town."

As an important part of Wenzhou City, Ouhai District contributes an important share in the city's clothing industry and other traditional industries, which lays a very good foundation for the realization of the "Fashion Manufacturing" concept. Relying on a solid light-industrial base, it has actively built a fashion design platform to promote design innovation, complete with the construction of a "University Creative Pioneer Park" and a "Guozhi Cultural Industry Creative Park," which also forms a gathering area for the future "Ouhai Cultural and Creative Design" venture. It also depends on the "Wenzhou University City" and the "University Science Park" to deepen the cooperation between industry and academics, and to boost the fashion industry innovation and entrepreneurship.

According to the plan, Ouhai Fashion Manufacturing Town will be located at Xianyan streets near the South Gate of Wenzhou City, which covers an area of about 2. 8 square kilometers. It consists of one axis called the Fashion Function Axis, two zones which are Fashion Production Zone and Fashion Living Zone, three areas known as Fashion Vitality Area, Fashion Intellectual Area, and the E-commerce Area, and twelve workshops. For example, the Fashion Wedding Workshop, has a total investment of proximately 700 million yuan, and mainly uses the surrounding countryside scenery, and its cultural and educational resources to create a wedding photography base, a hotel with catering services and other wedding facilities. Another workshop is the Fashion Shopping Mall, with a total of 300 acres of land, which mainly houses fashion shoes, clothing industries, clothing factories, Cloud experience shops, and clothing boutiques.

In order to better construct the town, the Ouhai District has made good use of its profound cultural heritage. With its deep historical background, the representative of the Yongjia School, Chen Fuliang, set up the earliest academy in southern Zhejiang to promote the doctrine that "Knowledge must be beneficial to state affairs" in the Southern Song Dynasty. The literary master Zhu Ziqing wrote the famous prose *Green*, which has long been a household name. In addition, the Ouhai District has an advantage of broad interpersonal connection, which creates an important guarantee for the development of the small town. In Paris, Milan, Rome, and New York, many Wenzhou people are at the fashion forefront, by displaying fashion information all over the world. In Ningbo, Shanghai, and Guangzhou, many Wenzhou people are agents of the well-known international brands. In the Haining Leather City, Hangzhou Sijiqing Market, Wenzhou businessmen are also everywhere. If Wenzhou people, in the area of fashion, were congregated, it would be the largest capital and power of the construction of the town.

In the near future, the Ouhai Fashion Manufacturing Town will be the main platform for the fashion industries in Wenzhou City and the good habitat for the innovative business-startup talents, thus becomes an iconic fashion industry base for the "Chinese Textile and Apparel Brand Center City".

# 瓯海时尚智造小镇

温州作为中国民营经济发展的先发地区与改革开放的前沿阵地，其成熟的制造业早已闻名国内外。近年来，为适应经济新常态，促进产业由"制造"向"智造"转型，推动传统产业向时尚产业升级，温州市委市政府提出了建设"时尚之都"战略。温州瓯海区抓住特色小镇建设的机遇，根据温州市和瓯海区现有的工业基础设施和产业发展方向，提出了建设瓯海时尚智造小镇的设想。

作为温州市重要组成部分的瓯海区，在全市服装等传统产业中占有重要份额，对于建设时尚智造小镇有着非常良好的基础。为建设瓯海时尚智造小镇，瓯海依托雄厚的轻工业基础，积极打造时尚设计平台，促进设计创新；同时还建设了温州市大学创意创业园、国智文化产业创意园等，形成未来瓯海文化创意和设计服务集聚区；同时依托温州大学城、大学科技园，深化产、学、研合作，学城联动、产城互动助推时尚产业创新创业。

根据规划，瓯海时尚智造小镇选址在温州市区南大门仙岩街道，占地面积约2.8平方千米。依照一轴（时尚功能轴）两带（时尚生产带、时尚生活带）三区（时尚活力区、时尚智造区、电子商贸区）十二坊的布局，实现轴带拉动、有机成长和产镇结合。例如，时尚婚博园，总投资约7亿元，主要利用周边乡村风光、文化教育资源，打造婚纱摄影基地、酒店餐饮服务等婚庆配套服务设施，形成独特的婚礼主题公园。时尚购物广场项目，总投资10亿元至12亿元，主要依托小镇时尚鞋服产业，打造服饰工厂、云定制体验店、服饰精品店等为载体的时尚购物广场。

为了更好地建设小镇,瓯海时尚智造小镇充分利用其所在的仙岩街道深厚的文化底蕴:南宋永嘉学派代表人陈傅良在此开办了浙南最早的书院,宣扬"经世致用"学说;文学大师朱自清在梅雨潭写下了散文名篇《绿》,"仙岩绿"早已家喻户晓。此外,瓯海区广泛的人脉资源优势,为小镇的发展提供了重要保障:在巴黎、米兰、罗马和纽约,许多温州人触及时尚前沿,掌握着世界各地的时尚信息;在宁波、上海和广州,许多国际知名品牌的代理商都是温州人;在海宁皮革城、杭州四季青市场,温州商人也无处不在。如果能够使全球做时尚产业的温州人资源汇聚起来、互动起来,它将是城市建设中最大的资本和力量。

在不久的将来,瓯海时尚智造小镇必将成为温州市时尚产业发展的主要平台,成为创新创业人才的良好栖息地,成为"中国纺织服装品牌中心城市"的标志性时尚产业基地。

# Cangnan Taiwanese Town

The Cangnan Taiwanese Town is located in the east of Chenglingxi Town, Cangnan County. It gets the name because of the fact that Cangnan has a long history of trading with Taiwan. In 2011, Cangnan set up the first provincial Economic and Trade Cooperation Zone with Taiwan, which led to more frequent interaction between two sides. By June, 2015, Cangnan has not only received more than 3000 Taiwanese, but also introduced 27 Taiwan investment projects. In 2014, the "Cross-strait Ethnic Minority Exchanges and Cooperation Base" landed in Cangnan. After the initial few years, it paved the way for its own development. Cangnan has integrated into many Taiwan business ideas with its agriculture, tourism, early childhood education, cultural, and creative aspects. Hence, the Taiwanese Town comes into existence.

Cangnan Taiwanese Town is planned to cover an area of 2.7 square kilometers. Within 3 years, the six-block construction will be done. It will be not related to shopping malls, supermarkets, Taiwan snacks, or a series of retail goods as many people thought it would. In fact, the Taiwanese town identifies itself in the area of the "optoelectronics" industry. For example, in the eastern part of the town there is a building called the "Fuqi Industrial

Park" that is the Taiwan photoelectric supporting industrial base, the Nano Photoelectric Industry Base, Science and Technology Museum Exhibition Complex, and the Laser Supporting Industrial area. Located in the west of town, there is the Taiwan Photoelectric Information Park and Business District. In December, 2014, Cangnan county government signed a "Strategic Framework Agreement" with the Foxconn Fuqi Investment and Development Co., Ltd., who will invest 12 billion yuan into the photoelectric industry in three phases from 2015 to 2020. Their focus is on scientific and technological research of information, high-end optoelectronic materials, optoelectronic and optics talent cultivation.

In addition to a series of photoelectric industries, the Taiwanese town has residential areas, leisure squares, the "Taiwan Snack Streets," tourism distribution centers, the "Taiwan Style Wetland Tourism Park" and other supporting facilities. A staff member of the Taiwanese town's project headquarter named Renjie said, "The wetland tourism park fully expresses the distinctive characteristics of Taiwan. People who visit here will think they have arrived at a condensed version of Taiwan. The entrance to the sightseeing park is located in the northwestern corner of the town, while the whole landscape is distributed along the meandering river." In accordance with the plan, the sightseeing park has condensed all of the Taiwan traditional customs, such as flowers and trees that are planted in the method used by the Taiwanese. It is also embedded in the Southern Fujian exotic atmosphere and the Matsu Culture landscape.

What's more, around the town, there will also be a "Taiwan style tourism zone." For example, "Sun-Moon Lake Farm" "Shangtai Alishan Farm" "Zhejiang, Fujian and Taiwan National Flower Ecological Park" and more. In Xiaguan, "A Trade Logistics Park for Taiwan" "Taiwan Commodity Trading Market" "Taiwan Wholesale Fruit Market" and "Cross-Strait Aquatic Products Processing and Distribution Base" will be prepared for construction. In short, this series of external supports can help Cangnan Taiwanese Town form a more open pattern, and strengthen its external interaction.

# 苍南台商小镇

　　规划中的台商小镇位于苍南县城灵溪镇城东区域,为何被定名为"台商小镇"? 它得名的原因是苍南与中国台湾有着悠久的贸易关系。2011 年,苍南与中国台湾就建立了浙江省首个对台经贸合作区。随着两地频繁的互动,到 2015 年 6 月,苍南已接待访苍台湾人士3000多人了,还落地了 27 个台商投资项目,同时两岸少数民族交流合作基地登陆苍南,霞关成为对台小额贸易点。通过这几年的发展,苍南的农业、旅游、幼教、文化创意各方面都融入了台商理念,台商小镇也顺理成章地应运而生。

　　台商小镇规划占地面积约 2.7 平方千米,计划在 3 年内建成六大区块,台商小镇不是很多人想象的那样——一个集商场、超市、台湾小吃等一系列零售商品的交易地,而是以光电、光学产业为主的小镇。例如,小镇东部四块区域分别是富奇工业园(中国台湾光电配套产业基地)、纳米光电产业基地、科技体验馆会展综合体、激光配套产业区,小镇西部还有富奇工业园(中国台湾光电信息园)商贸区。2014 年 12 月,苍南县政府与富士康富奇投资开发有限公司签署了"战略框架协议",将于 2015 年至 2020 年期间,投资120 亿元投入光电产业,重点开展信息光电高端材料的科技研发、光电光学人才培育。

　　除了一系列光电产业,台商小镇还有住宅区、休闲广场、小吃街、旅游集散中心、"台湾风情湿地观光园"等配套设施,其中"台湾风情湿地观光园"充分体现了中国台湾的特色,观光公园的入口位于小镇的西北角,而整个景观沿着蜿蜒的河流分布,里面的花草树木,全部按照中国台湾的景观栽种,同时还融入了闽南风情、妈祖文化等景观,来到这里的人们会以为到了浓缩版的中国台湾。

此外,为了使来到这个城市的游客一眼就知道这是一个光电主题园区,在台商小镇周围,政府还将配套建立"台湾风情旅游观光带",比如,"日月潭农庄""尚台阿里山农庄""浙闽台民族花海生态园"等。在霞关,还将筹建"对台贸易物流园""台湾小商品交易市场""台湾水果批发市场"等。

# Huzhou

湖 州

# Huzhou Silk Town

Huzhou silk has a 4700-year history. Qianshanyang cultural relics are the strong evidence. From the Spring and Autumn periods to the Northern and Southern Dynasties, Huzhou Ling Silk was exported to more than 10 countries. In the Tang, Ming and Qing Dynasties, it became the national silk export center, and as the saying goes "tens of thousands of mulberries in Shu, millions of silk machines in Wu," it became a true expression. During the Ming Dynasty, Huzhou's "Jili Silk" became world-famous, while in the Qing Dynasty, its "Huzhou Silk" was regarded as the best quality in the country. In 1851, Huzhou Silk was the only product of China to win prize in the First World Exposition in London. In 1929, it was awarded the Grand Prize of the First West Lake Exposition.

Today, China has put forward the prospect of "The Belt and Road." With silk as an important product, Huzhou once again attracts the attention of the world. In 2015, Huzhou Silk Town was listed among the province's first 37 towns with characteristics. With an area about 3.55 square kilometers, it's divided into "two areas and two zones." The Display Area features silk cultural history, and the Gathering Area features elements of modern silk industry. The Silk

Production Demonstration Zone and the Silk Innovation Zone lie nearby. With "World Silk Source，World Silk Town" as the overall goal，it plans to create three functional centers，which will be the "International Silk Cultural Research Center," the "National Silk Products Trade Exhibition Center," and the "National Silk Product Design and Manufacturing Center."

In July，2016，the Huzhou Silk Town Planning Conference was held in Hangzhou. A total of 300 silk industry leaders，silk town cooperation unit representatives，and news media gathered at the West Lake. On the ceremony site，a total of 31 companies signed agreements to prepare for settlement in the silk town. The projects involved silk creative design，silk product development，creative wedding，and other fields.

According to the plan，Huzhou Silk Town，with the concept of "Production，Living，Ecology," plans to spend 3 years building a "Silk Cultural and Creative Vacation Town" with a group of silk industries， historical relics, and tourism. At the same time, it will rely on research and design to achieve the entire industry chain development, while striving to build the Global Silk Fashion Design Center, the Silk Products Trading Center and the Silk Culture Experience Center.

The town follow the "Silk Road" legend by actively promoting a supply reform, speeding up industrial transformation and upgrading, and being committed to industrial service innovation.

# 湖州丝绸小镇

---

湖州丝绸有 4700 多年的历史,钱山漾文化遗址的出土文物就是强有力的佐证。从春秋时期到南北朝,湖州绫绢已经出口到 10 多个国家。在明清时期,湖州已成为国家丝绸出口中心,当时就有"蜀桑万亩,吴蚕万机"的说法。在明代,湖州的"辑里丝"闻名天下。而在清朝,其"湖丝"被认为是全国最好的。1851 年,湖州丝绸作为中国唯一产品参加伦敦首届世界博览会获大奖;1929 年,参加全国首届西湖博览会获特等奖。

多年后的今天,中国提出了"一带一路"的愿景,以丝绸为重要载体,湖州再次吸引了世界的关注。2015 年,湖州丝绸小镇被列入全省第一批 37 个特色小镇。湖州丝绸小镇总面积约 3.55 平方千米,分为两个片区:由北部西山漾片区和南部凌波塘片区组成,总体定位为"两地两区",即"丝绸文化历史的展示地、现代丝绸产业要素的集聚地、丝绸制造的示范区、丝绸创新创业的先行区",提出"世界丝源·天下绸都"的总体目标,打造三大功能中心——国际丝绸文化研究展示中心、国家丝绸产品交易展示中心和国家丝绸产品设计制造中心。

2016 年 7 月,湖州丝绸小镇规划发布会暨合作签约项目签约仪式在杭州举行,丝绸行业领军人物、丝绸小镇合作单位负责人和新闻媒体代表共 300 多人聚集在西湖。在仪式现场,共有 31 个项目签约入驻丝绸小镇,项目涉及丝绸创意设计、丝绸产品开发、创意婚礼等领域。

根据规划,湖州丝绸小镇将围绕"生产、生活、生态"的理念,计划花 3 年时间搭建一个"丝绸文创度假小镇",建设成为集丝绸产业、历史文物、主体旅游为一体的开放式小镇。同时,将依靠研究设计实现整个产业链的发展,努力打造全球丝绸时尚设计中心、丝绸产品交易中心和丝绸文化体验中心。

通过积极推进供应改革,加快产业转型升级,致力于产业服务创新,湖州丝绸小镇创造了"丝绸之路"的又一段传奇。

# Huzhou Writing Brush Town in Shanglian

Brush manufacturing in Shanlian Town has more than a 2000-year history. Generations of people here are engaged in the production of this traditional handmade brush. Because Shanlian is under Huzhou's jurisdiction, the brush is called the "Huzhou brush", which is also known as "the precious one" out of "four treasures for study" with Hui ink, Duan inkstone, and Xuan paper. It represents the highest development of the Chinese brush production.

According to the book *Ancient and Modern Annotation*, written during the Qin Dynasty, the great General Meng Tian created the brush with Zhe wood for the body and goat hair for the head. Therefore, the people who respect Meng Tian as the brush's father, continue making brushes in Meng Tian's way. Today, there exists 150 home workshops, with an annual output of 8 million brushes. Huzhou writing brushes share about 20% of the country's brush market, with the top-graded ones at 50%. Its related industries have an annual output value of 212 million yuan, which accounts for 12% of the GDP in the region.

In addition to the development of the Huzhou writing brush industry, Shanlian town also finds ways to maintain the native Huzhou writing brush culture and compiles its history to strengthen its protection. There are restorations of the ancestral temple of Meng Tian, a "Yongxin Temple" which is for the famous calligrapher of the southern Dynasty Zhiyong, Huzhou Writing brush Cultural Hall, Huzhou writing brush Street and Huzhou writing brush Factory in Shanlian. At the same time, through skill contests and other activities, one could enhance Huzhou writing brush production skills and strengthen the workforce. At present the town has one national non-material cultural heritage successor, four national masters, three provincial arts and crafts masters, and one municipal intangible cultural heritage successor.

In June, 2015, after the "Huzhou Writing Brush Town" was named among the first towns with special characteristics of Zhejiang Province, the Huzhou Brush Town began another "dream journey." Relying on southern China's special environment while holding tight to the essence of Huzhou culture, Shanlian Town will fully realize perfect grafting of the traditional protection and modern function development to create an innovative cultural tourism town with Huzhou writing brush cultural experience, cultural education training, health, and relaxation.

According to the plan, Huzhou writing Brush Town covers a range of 4.08 square kilometers, of which the core area is about 1.2 square kilometers. The town is divided into "three axes and four areas." The "three axes" include the Ecological Landscape Axis, the Cultural Experience Axis, and the Leisure Holiday Axis, while the "four areas" refer to the Huzhou writing Brush Industrial Gathering Area, the Town Cultural Touring Area, the Business Service Supporting Area, and the Leisure and Sightseeing Service Area. Through 3 to 5 years' development, Huzhou writing Brush Town aims to become China's Huzhou writing brush industry gathering place. A national painting and calligraphy art trade center, Zhejiang's cultural town demonstration base, a creative cultural experience tourism destination near the Yangtze River Delta, and a new tourism demonstration area are also planned to established at the town.

# 南浔善琏湖笔小镇

善琏镇制笔已有 2000 多年的历史，这里的人们一直从事毛笔制作这一古老的传统手工技艺。由于善琏镇在湖州辖区内，其制作的毛笔亦被叫作"湖笔"，与徽墨、端砚、宣纸一起被称为"文房四宝"，是中国毛笔制作发展到最高水平的产物。

根据西晋《古今注》中的说法，善琏人向来以做笔为谋生的手段，尊奉蒙恬为"笔祖"，其制作工艺，也一直秉承蒙恬之制法，且延续至今。今天，善琏湖笔产业也得到了蓬勃发展，现有 150 个家庭作坊，年产量 800 万支，国内毛笔市场占有率约为 20%，高档毛笔市场占有率为 50% 左右。其相关行业年产值达 2.12 亿元，占该地区生产总值的 12%。

除了湖笔产业的发展，善琏镇为了保持乡土文化的原生态，增强古迹保护，新修建了"一祠一寺一馆一街一厂"，即纪念笔祖蒙恬的蒙公祠，纪念王羲之七代孙、南朝著名书法家智永禅师的永欣寺，湖笔文化馆，湖笔一条街和善琏湖笔厂。同时，通过技能竞赛等活动，加强笔工队伍的建设，更好地传承湖笔制作工艺。目前，该镇有一个国家非物质文化遗产继承人，四位国家级制笔大师，三位省级工艺美术大师，一位市非物质文化遗产继承者。

2015 年 6 月，"湖笔小镇"成为浙江省首批特色小镇，古镇开始了另一个新的梦想之旅。依托江南水乡之境，国学文化之情，善琏镇立足湖笔文化资源品牌，充分实现传统风貌保护和现代功能开发的完美结合，打造集湖笔文化体验、国学文化研修、健康养生及休闲度假于一体的创新型文化旅游小镇。

湖笔小镇规划设计面积为 4.08 平方千米,其中核心区约 1.2 平方千米。该镇空间布局分为"三轴四区"。"三轴"包括生态景观轴、文化体验轴和休闲度假轴,"四个区"指湖笔工业集聚区、古镇文化旅游区、商贸配套服务区和休闲观光拓展服务区。经过 3 至 5 年的发展,湖笔小镇的目标是成为中国湖笔产业聚集地、全国书画艺术品交易中心、浙江特色文化小镇示范基地、长三角创意文化体验型旅游目的地和新型旅游拓展要素示范地。

# Deqing Geographic Information Town

An electronic navigation system is needed if people travel to an unfamiliar city. The number of parking spaces available should be checked if people park their cars. Metals are located and detected when people mine, and check the underground sewage pipe network for "healthiness," even if people don't dig the ground. It's like doing an ultrasound as a precaution in a hospital. This great application for geographic information is achieved now in the northern city of Zhejiang Province at the Deqing Geographic Information Town.

In 2015, the Deqing Geographic Information Town was selected as one of the Zhejiang provincial-level towns with special characteristics. On May 6th, at the Foundation Stone Laying Ceremony of the United Nations Global Geographic Information Management Deqing Forum, the international officials spoke highly of the Geographic Information Town, which indicated that the "Deqing Era" was coming. Today, in this three-square-kilometer town, 63 geographic information-related businesses have settled there. Deqing Geographic Information Town has become a code word for geographical information industries in the Yangtze River Delta area. The basis for the geographical cultural rising is that the culture changes the patterns of local people, and as time flies, changes their cultural characteristics as well.

Geographic information refers to data and images related to the quantity, quality, and nature of the geographic environment. Compared with the general public space projects, the geographic information project, as an "incubator" object, are more specialized and refined. They, based on modern surveying, mapping, and technological information, take geographic information development and utilization as the core, to reflect the spatial distribution of land surface and geographic location information in 2D, 3D and multidimensional ways. The advantages are high technology, less environmental pollution, good market prospect, and high employment rate. It is reported that 80% of human activity is geographically related. The United States and other developed countries regard geographic information technology as one of the three most important emerging areas in the 21st century. For example, the application of GPS, as the representative of satellite navigation, has become the world's third largest IT application after Mobile Communications and Internet, which IBM, Microsoft, Google, Yahoo, Apple and other international software giants have set foot on.

In the Deqing Geographic Information Town, intelligent pipeline robots, smart unmanned aerial vehicles, lightweight and convenient mapping equipment, and other geographic information products amazed people, but the most eye-catching is the first GIS professional public space called the "Geographic Information Dream Works." After several months of exploration, the second phase of the project began being built with a 10000 square meter office space, which benefits professionals a lot. For example, on the 3rd floor of the "Geographic Information Dream Works," Guo Yi's team is busy debugging the Orange Map Application. This Internet map is specifically developed for overseas travel. At present, domestic use of map software generally does not contain foreign map details. It is what Guo Yi's team are doing. "Our goal is to expand the use of the map as a platform for social communication, entertainment and other

functions, which will provide more convenience for the overseas tourists." Guo Yi, who was collecting geographic information in Bangkok, Thailand, said she showed some people the "Orange Map" beta version, which displays a clear location of Kyrgyzstan. At present, the "Geographic Information Dream Works" has more than 20 entrepreneurial teams. Having cooperation with South China's TOPRS Technology Co., Ltd., and China's Zhenyuan Geomatics Co., Ltd. to hold technical exchanges and other activities from time to time has been beneficial.

"The Geographic Information Dream Works not only provides a wide range of services for the settled venture team, but also offers professional services to help them find capital, technologies, markets, and talents to build the dream together," Chen Yiping, Director of the Administrative Committee for the Science and Technology Park, stated. The "Intelligent Water Management Cloud" platform, and the "Wisdom City Project" are the crystallization of their cooperation. In Deqing's rural construction, there was a big problem about how sewage pipe emissions could be monitored in real time. When Shen Jingliang learned about this, he immediately contacted scientific research entrepreneurial teams and several enterprises to jointly deliver the solution. The "Xihe System" entrepreneurial team, from the Technology Transfer Center at Wuhan University, was to solve "the last kilometer" issues of the Global Satellite Navigation System, which is related to mutual integration of communication, remote sensing, mobile internet and other industries. Guo Chi, one of the team members, said, "Relying on the Geographic Information Town, it makes easy to find the adjacent industrial chain to facilitate business work. At present, the Xihe System we developed has established four ground-strengthening stations in Deqing for town enterprises to provide free signal distribution services of outdoor high-precision positioning."

The "Geographic Information Dream Works" is an open and shared public space. Here, relying on the cluster effect, industries are undergoing the metamorphosis to promote its development in breadth and depth. In the future, the development of geographic information industries in Deqing will boost the development of a series of industries such as Wisdom Education, Wisdom Medical Care, Wisdom Tourism, which will provide the strongest support and guarantee for a better intellectual life.

# 德清地理信息小镇

————————

来到一个陌生的城市需要电子地图导航,停车时需要查看有无空余车位;采矿时需要检测金属含量和定位,检查地下污水管网是否"健康",即使不挖地,也可像医院做 B 超那样简单……这些先进的地理信息应用技术,在浙江省北部城市德清就能实现。

2015 年,德清地理信息小镇被列入了浙江省省级特色小镇创建名单。同年 5 月 6 日,在联合国全球地理信息管理德清论坛奠基仪式上,国际专家高度评价了地理信息小镇德清,这表明一个关于地理信息产业的"德清时代"已经来临。在这约 3 平方千米的地理小镇上,63 家地理信息相关企业纷纷落户,德清地理信息小镇已渐渐成为长江三角洲地理信息产业的一个代名词,在此基础上产生的地理文化正逐渐改变着当地人的原有文化格局,并随着时间的推进,小镇独树一帜的文化气质正在形成。

地理信息是指与地理环境的数量、质量、性质有关的数据和图像。与一般公共空间项目相比,地理信息项目作为孵化器的对象,更加专业化、精细化。他们基于现代测绘技术信息,以地理信息开发利用为核心,通过二维、三维和多维的方式将地表空间分布和地理位置相关的信息反映出来,具有环境污染少、技术含量高和高就业率的良好市场前景。据报道,人类活动的80%的信息是和地理信息相关的。美国等发达国家将地理信息技术视为21 世纪最重要的新兴领域之一。例如,以 GPS 应用为代表的卫星导航市场,正在成为继移动通信和互联网之后的全球第三大 IT 经济新增长点,国际软件巨头 IBM、微软、谷歌、雅虎、苹果等纷纷涉足该产业。

在德清地理信息小镇里，智能管道机器人、智能无人驾驶汽车、轻巧方便的测绘设备和其他地理信息产品让人感到惊讶，但最引人注目的是国内第一家地理信息专业众创空间"地信梦工场"。经过几个月的探索，该项目的第二阶段将开始，约有 1 万平方米办公场所的众创空间将在这里建成。为专业的人提供专业的服务，才能让地信梦想起航。例如，在三楼的"地理信息梦工程"中，郭艺团队正忙着调试"桔子地图"应用程序，这个互联网地图是专门为海外旅行而开发的。目前，国内使用的地图软件一般不包含外国地图的细节。发布一款针对海外旅游的地图应用程序作为社会交流、娱乐等功能的平台，为海外游客提供更多的便利，这是郭艺的团队正在做的。目前，"地信梦工场"已有 20 多个创业团队入驻，并和地信小镇内的中测新图、南方测绘、正元地信等企业建立了合作意向，举行不定期的技术交流、路演等活动。

"地信梦工场"不仅为入驻的创业团队提供范围广泛的服务，还为企业和青年提供专业的服务，帮助他们找资金、技术、市场、人才，共筑梦想。智能水管理云平台、智慧城市项目正是各方合作的结晶。在德清"美丽乡村"建设中，如何对污水管排放进行实时监测，成为当时一大难题。"地信梦工场"的科研创业团队与入驻小镇的其他企业合作，共同研发出了解决方案。武汉大学技术转移中心的"羲和系统"创业团队，要解决全球卫星导航系统"最后一千米"的问题，这需要通讯、遥测遥感、移动互联网等产业的相互融合。依托地理信息小镇，很容易找到相邻的产业链，目前，"羲和系统"已经在德清建立了地基增强站，为小镇企业免费提供室外亚米级高精度定位信号播发服务。

"地信梦工场"是一个开放共享的新型众创空间。在这里，依托集群效应，产业正在经历蜕变，地信产业也在向广度和深度发展。在未来，德清地理信息产业的发展必将推动智慧教育、智慧医疗、智慧旅游等一系列产业的发展，为美好的智慧生活提供支持保障。

# Jiaxing

嘉 兴

# Nanhu Fund Town

In the United States, Sand Hill Road is a fascinating place, where a large number of financial elites have gathered. It is notable for its concentration of venture capital companies and has become a synonym for that industry. Now in Jiaxing city, Zhejiang Province, a Chinese version of "Sand Hill Road" is also rising. It is called the Nanhu Fund Town.

The Nanhu Fund Town, located near the Hangzhou Bay and the southeast region of Jiaxing City, covers an area of about 2.04 square kilometers, with its rectangular distribution from north to south. Similar to Sand Hill Road, which is adjacent to Stanford University and Silicon Valley, the Nanhu Fund Town is only 30 minutes away by high-speed train from China's international financial center Shanghai. In 2014, the first World Internet Conference was held in Jiaxing which provided an opportunity for the development of Nanhu. The arrival of Jack Ma, Pony Ma, Robin Li, and many other great men of the internet industry brought great fame to the town. Thus, the town has become deeply associated with the internet. It cooperates with the industry elites to jointly establish the Nanhu Internet Financial Association, the Nanhu Credit Information Sharing Platform, the

Nanhu Internet Financial Innovation Center, and the Nanhu Internet Financial Investment Fund, to promote the development of an Internet financial industry.

In Zhejiang Province, Jiaxing has become a financial innovation sample. However, the Nanhu Fund Town is not limited to the internet. It has also actively expanded the investment circle and so the "Fund Town-Investment Circle" is born. The investment cycle platform construction is divided into two steps: the first step is to do some government investment and real estate projects, in order to offer an information release and exchange platform to financing enterprises, government financing entities, real estate developers and investment companies. The second step is to establish an equity investment circle network based on science and technology-based enterprises. The Nanhu Fund Town organizes the meeting of investment sides to carry out various lectures. Through the creating of a professional team, it provides professional training for enterprises on how to prepare in the market. In addition, if technology companies have the financing needs, the circle will also provide "one-to-one" docking services, recommendation of investment institutions, and make an appointment for face-to-face exchanges. After several years of development and cultivation, the Nanhu Fund Town has achieved certain results in attracting investment industry agglomeration and serving real economic development in the region.

To attract funds, the Nanhu Fund Town has also focused on the service environment, the credit environment, the integrity of the government, and other soft environments, in hopes of providing

comprehensive, efficient and convenient services for enterprises. The Nanhu District has specifically set up service sectors for their settled Internet financial institutions, such as a full and free set of administrative examinations and approval procedures to provide registration, change, or open an account. In view of the special nature of the registration for partnership enterprises, its staff has actively coordinated with the departments, opening up a " Green Channel" of the fund registration for enterprises to provide "one-stop" services.

Besides the convenient administrative services, the Nanhu District is also considerate of other aspects. For example, in the design of office environment, the town integrates southern China's culture into the planning and architectural style of the Fund Town. As a hardware assurance, it combines natural advantages with the layout of a large area of green and water landscape, which makes living areas and business facilities more comfortable.

By creating a platform that gathers capital, technology, talent and other high-end factors, the Nanhu Fund Town has gradually formed a strong financial atmosphere, and become a model town with happy living and working condition.

# 南湖基金小镇

在美国,沙山路是一个让人心驰神往的地方,许多金融精英聚居于此,它是创业者的圣地,也是风险投资的代名词。如今在浙江嘉兴,一个中国版的"沙山路"也正在崛起,它的名字叫作南湖基金小镇。

南湖基金小镇,位于杭州湾畔,嘉兴市东南区域,小镇规划占地约 2.04 平方千米,呈南北向狭长形的长方形分布。嘉兴市的地理环境和美国的沙山路非常相似,距离中国的国际金融中心上海,高铁车程只有 30 分钟。于是,南湖区决定借鉴沙山路的模式,做一个中国版的基金小镇。2014 年首届世界互联网大会的举办给嘉兴提供了发展契机,马云、马化腾、李彦宏等众多互联网大鳄的到来,让这座低调温婉的江南小城一时间声名鹊起。而更让嘉兴人骄傲的是,嘉兴被官方指定为世界互联网大会的永久会址。南湖区作为嘉兴市的重要组成部分,与互联网产生了格外深厚的联系。它携手业界精英,共同成立南湖互联网金融学会、南湖互联网金融创业中心、南湖征信数据共享平台、南湖互联网金融投资基金等,以促进互联网金融业的发展。

在浙江省,南湖基金小镇已成为金融创新的样本。然而,小镇不局限于拥抱互联网,它还积极拓展投融圈,"基金小镇—投融圈"应时而生。该投融圈平台建设分为两步走:第一步是做一些政府投资项目和房地产项目,为股权融资企业、政府融资平台、房地产开发投资企业提供信息发布和交流平台;第二步是建立以科创型企业为主的股权投融圈网。南湖基金小镇将组织投融双方的对接会,通过建立专业团队,为企业提供上市前的准备和上市后的市值管理等培训。此外,如果科技企业有融资需求,投融圈也将提供"一对一"对接服务,推荐投资机构,并预约双方进行面对面交流。经过几年的发展和培育,南湖基金小镇在吸引投资产业集聚和服务区域实体经济发展等方面取得了一定成效。

为吸引基金入驻,南湖基金小镇加强了在投资软环境的打造,希望为入驻企业提供全程、全面和高效便捷的服务。为此,专门设立了为互联网金融机构落户运营的服务部门,设专人免费为互联网金融机构提供注册、变更、开户等全套行政审批手续。针对合伙企业注册登记的特殊性,工商、税务等部门专门开辟基金注册登记的"绿色通道",为企业提供"一站式"全程服务。

除了加强在投资软环境上的打造外,南湖区还从各方面用心谋划,如在办公环境的设计中,小镇将水乡文化融入基金小镇的规划和建筑风格中,作为营造文化氛围的硬件保障。同时,小镇结合天然的自然优势,布局大面积的绿化、水景景观、环绕办公区、生活区,使人犹如置身在自然之中。

南湖基金小镇通过打造资本、技术、人才等高端要素集聚的平台,形成金融氛围浓厚、特色鲜明、集聚效应凸显的"乐居、乐活、乐业"的特色示范型小镇。

# Jiashan Sweet Town of Chocolates

"Looking out from the Bucket's windows, you can see the world's largest chocolate factory—Wonka chocolate. It is a mysterious factory producing and selling Wonka chocolates around the world, being deeply loved by children. A little boy called Charlie, in every night, dreamed that he could enter the factory..." Many years later, the scene in the film *Charlie and the Chocolate Factory* was still deeply craved in Mo Xuefeng's heart, who stated, "I am just like that little boy. The difference between us is that when I grew up, I turned the dream into reality."

Mo Xuefeng's town of chocolates—"AFICION" was set up at the southern tip of Jiashan County. It is not only a chocolate factory but also a theme park, for in addition to seeing the whole process of chocolate production, people can taste all kinds of chocolates in the DIY kitchens. What's more, there are "Chocolate Academies, Coco Forests," film production bases, and so on. "Do nothing but the best" is the slogan of the town. So Mo Xuefeng imported the best raw materials from other countries, such as, Californian almonds and cocoa beans, Turkey's hazelnuts, West African and South American cocoa beans, New Zealand milk, and the United States milk. Then he explored the most suitable chocolate recipe for Chinese people in a Swiss laboratory. But that's not exactly the entire story. In order to produce chocolates of the highest quality, Mo Xuefeng introduced from Switzerland the first-class production equipment, and built the world's top chocolate production lines. To allow visitors to see the whole process of chocolate production, he built a 156-meter long transparent channel in "AFICION," so visitors can have a panoramic view of the chocolate production line that was imported from Switzerland. The unique sightseeing channel allows tourists to directly experience the production process, which cultivates the intimacy of tourists and chocolates.

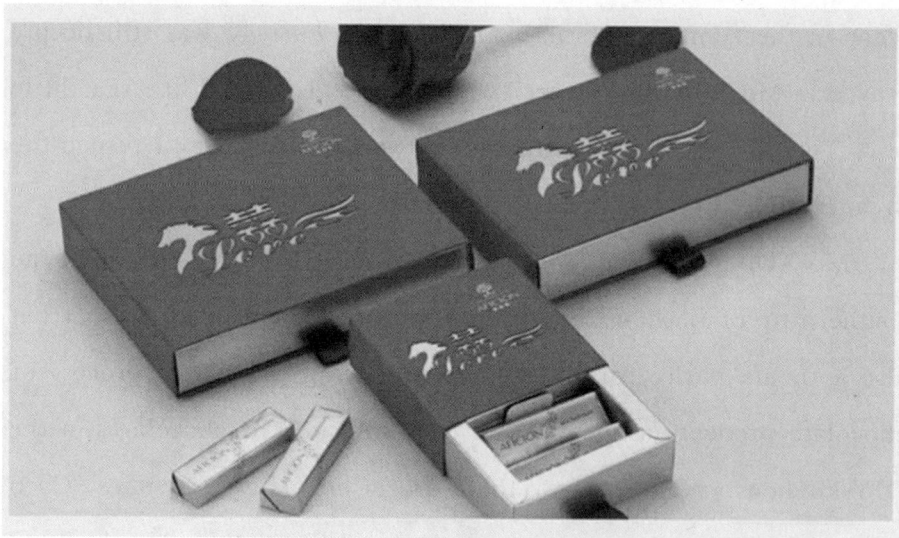

The town not only introduces the matured industrial tourism mode, but also pays attention to the cultivation of innovation, expanding the chocolate industrial production into chocolate industrial tourism, chocolate cultural creativity, and chocolate community life, which combines China traditional culture with foreign culture.

In order to highlight the positioning and features of the chocolate town, at present, in accordance with 5A scenic standards, the Chocolate Town features a construction planning site of 3 square kilometers, a core area design scheme, and its industrial development planning site. At the same time, the town fully enhances its infrastructure, including road construction, tourist traffic control, and environmental protection.

Among the first characteristic towns in Zhejiang Province, the sweet and romantic town will stick to the joint development of ecology, industries and tourism. The experiential town with industrial tourism, cultural creation, and romantic style begins to take shape. To make the exotic culture rooted in the mainland, there is still a long way to go. Will this chocolate town become "China's sweetest place"? Let us wait and see.

# 嘉善巧克力甜蜜小镇

"从巴克特一家的窗子望出去,可以看到全世界最大的巧克力工厂——旺卡巧克力工厂。那是座神秘的工厂,出产的旺卡牌巧克力销往世界各地,深受孩子们的喜爱。小男孩查理,在每个夜晚的梦乡中,都幻想自己可以亲身进入那座工厂……"很多年后,莫雪峰的心里仍然深深地渴望着电影《查理和巧克力工厂》的场景,他就像那个小男孩,所不同的是,长大后,他把梦想变为了现实。

莫雪峰的歌斐颂巧克力小镇位于嘉善县南端,它不仅是一个巧克力工厂,还是一个主题乐园。在这里除了可以看到巧克力生产的整个过程,品尝各种口味和造型的巧克力以外,还可以参观巧克力学院、可可森林、电影制作等基地。"要么不做,要做就做最好的"是嘉善巧克力甜蜜小镇的口号。为此,莫雪峰带着团队从各地引进最好的原材料,如加利福尼亚的杏仁和可可豆、土耳其的榛子等。同时又从国外引进了巧克力"mini"生产线,让游客定制一份专属于自己的巧克力,甚至在巧克力上画他们的名字。为了让游客能够看到巧克力生产的全过程,莫雪峰还在小镇里建造了一条长达156米的透明通道,游客可以清楚地看到从瑞士进口的巧克力生产线全景,这条观光通道在世界上是独一无二的,游客可以直接体验生产过程,培养游客和巧克力的亲密关系。小镇不但引进了国外成熟的工业旅游模式,而且在此基础上还着力创新,将巧克力工业生产拓展为巧克力工业旅游、巧克力文化创意、巧克力社区生活,而且还积极将中国传统文化与国外风情文化相结合,在浓郁的可可香味中体验迷人的热带风情和西非文化。

为了突出巧克力小镇的定位和特色,目前,小镇正在按照5A级旅游景区标准编制特色小镇约3平方千米控制性建设规划、核心区约1平方千米的城市设计方案及小镇产业发展规划。同时,全镇将全力提升小镇基础设施配套,包括道路建设、旅游交通、环境整治等方面的内容。

作为浙江省37个首批创建的省级特色小镇之一,巧克力小镇围绕甜蜜和浪漫两大主题,坚守生态底色、旅游主线,一个集工业旅游、文化创意、浪漫风情为一体的体验式小镇已经初现雏形。将巧克力这种外来的文化植根在本土,还有很长的路要走,巧克力小镇会成为"中国最甜蜜的地方"吗?让我们拭目以待。

# Haiyan Nuclear Power Town

Haiyan County is the birthplace of nuclear power in mainland China and it is where the Qinshan Nuclear Power Station that China first designed and constructed located. Based on the advantage of the Qinshan Nuclear Power Base, and China's nuclear power town construction, the Qinshan government has developed nuclear power associated industries, and thus built the Nuclear Power Town.

The Hanyan Nuclear Power Town covers an area of about 3.305 square kilometers, with an orientation of developing the high-end equipment manufacturing industry, which belongs to Zhejiang Province's seven key industries of the future. It focuses on nuclear-related industries, highlighting the development of nuclear power production services, nuclear power equipment manufacturing, and nuclear power tourism. By the end of 2015, the Nuclear Power Town had partly achieved an investment of more than 2 billion yuan. 98 enterprises had been settled, including more than forty nuclear power related enterprises.

In addition to the nuclear power industry as a strong support, the Nuclear Power Town has featured "Organic Integration of Industrial Tourism" "Leisure Agriculture" and a "beautiful countryside." After the Qinshan Nuclear

Power Station was awarded in 2004 the title of "National Industrial Tourism Demonstration" by China's National Tourism Administration, the Qinshan Nuclear Power Science and Technology Museum started to be constructed. It was built at the Yangtze River Delta, which is a famous tourist destination, so the country's first nuclear power technology tourism area was created as a national 4A-class tourism attraction. There will also be a nuclear power observation tower at the seaside that has the touring function of watching the sea, the nuclear power plant, and a cross-sea bridge, which is going to be an important landmark in northern Zhejiang after completion. In addition, while relying on the rich ecological tourism resources, the Nuclear Power Town will also be associated with the beautiful rural village Wenxi Dock, the Wentuan Village, the ecological park Wan'ao Farm, the Xixi vegetable garden, and the largest archipelago, White Tower islands in the north of Zhejiang Province. Other tourism resources will add brilliance to the town.

Taking advantage of the Chinese Red Tourism Base, the Nuclear Power Town, with the Binhai Harmony Cultural Avenue as the main axis, focuses on developing a "Nuclear Culture Tourism" industry. On one hand, there is the peaceful use of nuclear energy, with nuclear power knowledge that is shown to promote the development of nuclear power science and technology tourism. On the other hand, the quiet ecological environment is combined with cultural atmosphere, which leads to the development of rural leisure tourism. With modern science and technology as the support, this nuclear power town will accumulate more rich historical and cultural deposits, which will certain radiate its vigor.

# 海盐核电小镇

海盐县是中国大陆核电的发源地,中国首次自己设计和建造的秦山核电站就坐落在海盐县的秦山街道。基于秦山核电基地和中国核电城镇建设的优势,秦山政府顺势而为,发展核电关联产业,建设核电特色小镇。

海盐核电小镇规划占地面积约 3.305 平方千米,产业定位属浙江省未来七大重点发展行业中的高端装备制造业,着重于核电相关产业,突出发展核电生产性服务业、核电装备制造业和核电工业科技旅游产业。截至 2015 年底,核电小镇已累计完成投资 20 多亿,有 90 多家企业落户,其中核电关联企业 40 多家。

除了强大的核电关联产业做支撑,核电小镇的特色还在于将工业旅游、休闲农业及"美丽乡村"点缀其中,将第一、第二、第三产业有机融合。2004 年秦山核电站被国家旅游局授予"国家级工业旅游示范点"称号,同时秦山核电科技馆开工建设,将成为浙北旅游明珠、长三角著名旅游地、国内首个核电工业科技旅游区,从而创建成国家 4A 级旅游景区。小镇还将在海边建设一座核电瞭望塔,兼具望海、观核电厂和观跨海大桥的游览功能,建成后将是浙北重要的标志性建筑。此外,依靠丰富的生态旅游资源,核电小镇将与美丽乡村文溪坞、北团村、生态园区万奥农庄、嬉溪菜园子休闲农业产业园,以及浙北地区离岸最近、面积最大的白塔山岛群和隐马山废弃石矿等旅游资源相结合,让核电小镇锦上添花。

围绕核电"国之光荣"的中国红色旅游基地品牌,以滨海和谐文化大道为主轴线的核电小镇,将重点发展核电文化旅游产业。一方面,以和平利用核能、普及核电知识等为特色,促进核电工业科技旅游业;另一方面,将幽静的生态环境与深厚的文化气息相结合,推动农村休闲旅游发展。以现代科技为背景,加之浓郁的历史文化底蕴,核电小镇必将焕发活力。

# Haining Fashionable Leather Town

From "It is Haining where China's leather is!" to "I look at the world, while fashion is led by me!", the advertising language has highlighted Haining leather's development and glorious history for 20 years. Today the traditional industry is experiencing a transformation and upgrading in order to become a world-class leather trade center. With major government investment in high-tech industries, the city has been steadily moving up in China's leather industry chain. In recent years, there have been fashion leather companies that move their design centers to Haining. Some companies even move their headquarters to that city. The change in Haining can be seen from its designers and business managers and how they plan the future of this town. Sun Haitao, a famous designer, is one of the examples in leather circles. In 2010, Sun Haitao had his first contact with Haining leather, and thought how it was completely different from the clothing design he used to do. There are so many limitations in leather materials, but as a designer he was willing to accept the challenge. Sun Haitao decided to take the chance. He bought a cabin there to allow his imaginations to run wild. In 2011, he proposed breaking the simplicity of leather and fur, and tried to "mix and match" leather and fur with cashmere, fabrics, silk, and lace, which attracted the attention of CCTV. Differing from most designers in the town, Sun Haitao has made the design process a service platform. His Haitao Company, with a team of more than 60 people, does all the business centered on the design, such as providing product positioning, brand planning, style design and other services.

Today more than 600 enterprises have designers with professional training, no less than 300 people have deeply rooted in the land. In 2015 China Leather Fashion Week, more than 1200 sets of new clothing was released to attract domestic and foreign professional customers, with 40000 transactions. This is the eighth year that the Leather Town held the annual fashion event. At the product launching conference, creative designs in the cabin finally become actual productions on the exhibition. "The constant introduction of industrial designers and studios is our long-term security to enhance leather manufacturing design and standards," said Wang Honghui, who is the Deputy General Manager of the town. Leather Fashion Week, Designer Contest, Popular Trend Release are becoming Haining's fashion labels.

Haining Leather City has also established strategic cooperation with the China Academy of Art, and 11 other design institutes to provide professional design services to upgrade their products, and to contribute a business philosophy. They also joined with the Zhejiang University of Technology to establish the first design consulting platform in China.

# 海宁皮革时尚小镇

从"中国皮革看海宁"到"我看世界，风尚看我"的广告语，见证着嘉兴市海宁皮革 20 多年的发展变迁和辉煌历史。今天，海宁皮革传统工业正在经历转型和升级，小镇以打造世界级的皮革时尚策源地和贸易服务中心、传统产业转型升级的示范基地为目标，计划三年总投资 58.9 亿元。随着政府对高科技产业的投资，中国皮革产业一直在稳步上升。近年来，由于海宁在产业链中的地位不断攀升，许多皮革时尚企业将他们的设计中心、制版中心设在海宁，一些公司甚至将总部和整个公司搬到了小镇。

添上"时尚"两字的传统皮革城会变成什么模样？看看扎根在海宁中国皮革城的设计师、企业主和管理者如何谋划小镇的未来，你就能知道。著名设计师孙海涛就是例子之一。2010 年，孙海涛第一次接触海宁皮装，"这和我以前做的服装设计是完全不同的，皮革的材质有很多的局限性，但作为设计师就应该接受挑战"。孙海涛决定试一试。在"皮革城"，他在自己的设计小木屋中，发挥奇思妙想。2011 年，海宁举办皮革时装周的时候，他提出要打破皮革皮草的单一性，推出混搭理念：把皮革皮草和羊绒呢料、真丝蕾丝混搭，发布的时候还引起了央视的关注。和"皮革城"大多数设计师不同，孙海涛把设计做成了服务平台，他的海涛时尚创意公司，已有 60 多人，所有的业务围绕设计来做，为"皮革城"的皮革制造企业提供产品定位、品牌策划、款式研发、风格培育等服务。

今天，海宁已拥有"科班出身"设计师的企业不少于 600 家，扎根海宁的设计师不少于 300 人。在 2015 年中国皮革时装周上,发布了 1200 多套服装新款,吸引国内外专业客商、买手 4 万人次,这是皮革城连续第八年举办年度时尚盛会了。在这场发布会上,那些曾躺在设计小木屋的创意之作终于成为实物走上舞台。持续引进行业内优秀的设计师、工作室,提升海宁皮革制造的设计含量和水准,这是海宁长期稳固发展的核心保障,而皮革时装周、设计师大赛、流行趋势发布正在成为海宁产业的时尚标签。

为了加快海宁皮革工业设计的发展,海宁皮革城已经与中国美术学院等 11 家设计院校建立战略合作,为生产企业提供专业设计服务,引领企业产品和经营理念升级。同时,还联合浙江理工大学,建立了中国皮革行业首个设计咨询平台。随着"设计＋"元素的融合,海宁中国皮革、裘皮服装展也有了新秀台,海宁皮革时尚小镇也将扬帆远航。

# Tongxiang Fashionable Sweater Town

The Fashionable Sweater Town is located in the eastern part of Puyuan Town, Tongxiang City. Puyuan Town, nearly 900-year-old town, was famous for the silk industry in the Ming and Qing Dynasties. At present, the ancient town still maintains the old building styles that are well-known in coastal areas along the Yangtze River. Pu Chuan's eight scenic spots still leave a good impression upon today's visitors, especially those well-preserved bridges that were rebuilt in the Southern Song and Qing dynasties, many of which are included in the heritage conservation units. Those with a high historical, artistic and cultural values, provide a prerequisite for founding the fashionable and cultural sweater town.

In 1978, with the "Chinese Economic Reform Policy," Puyuan seized the opportunity to dig out the first bucket of gold. One Tongxiang County-affiliated enterprise—Puyuan cooperatives purchased three sets of hand-knitting machines to produce woven shirts and then polypropylene sweaters, which set a good example for other units. Hence, the sweater industry came into being. After 40 years of development, the town has become the country's "Sweater Knitting Industrial Area" with the most complete industrial chain, realizing the improvement of the woolen sweater market and the knitting industrial park. In recent years, Puyuan actively participates in the fashionable areas, from issuing popular sweater trends to taking part in exhibitions in first-tier cities such as Shenzhen and Hong Kong, but the most important event in Puyuan is the annual "International Woolen Knitwear Exhibition" which displays the town's industrial and urban changes.

2016 China Puyuan Exhibition moved to Shanghai. With this exhibition, the Fashionable Sweater Town further expands its influence aggressively. It also attracted internet companies to bring their innovative driving force to the continuous development at the Puyuan Fashionable Sweater Town. They signed a contract with Busan Design Center in Korea, which lead to direct communication with Korean designing team, and 60 designers bringing the latest Korean popular designs.

It is understood that for the next three years, the Puyuan Sweater Town will invest 5. 5 billion in the cultural and creative sweater industries to promote real projects in Puyuan. From copying others' designs, to creating its own brand, to manufacturing, the Puyuan Fashionable Sweater Town will be a town with characteristics like knitted material development, fashion show release, and a tourism-driven town. At present, the town has more than 6000 sweater manufacturing enterprises, from spinning to dyeing to production with more than 10000 merchants and 0. 2 million employees. Three quarters of the town population are associated with this line of business. 90% of the Puyuan people's income are from sweater industry and related industries. In the future, it will come true. The goal of "Sweater Capital, Fashionable City" will be a reality. The Puyuan Sweater Town is moving forward.

# 桐乡毛衫时尚小镇

毛衫时尚小镇位于桐乡市濮院镇，这座拥有近900年历史的小镇，是明清时期著名的丝织业专业市镇和江南五大名镇之一。目前，古镇仍然保持在建时的建筑风格，名扬江南沿海地区。濮川八景更是留名千古，尤其是始建于南宋，重建于清道光年间的桥梁仍然保存完好，许多被列为文物保护单位，具有较高的历史、文化和艺术价值，为创建毛衫时尚小镇提供了历史文化条件。

1978年，随着中国经济改革的新政策，濮院人抓住机遇，挖掘了第一桶金。原桐乡县二轻总公司下属企业——濮院弹花生产合作社购买了3台手摇横机，摇织膨体衫，后又生产丙纶羊毛衫，诞生了第一件濮院羊毛衫，为其他单位树立一个好榜样，因此，毛衣行业应运而生。经过40多年的发展，该镇已具备全国羊毛衫针织产业领域最完整的产业链，实现了羊毛衫市场和针织工业园区的共同发展。近年来，濮院积极参与时尚领域，从四季毛针织服饰流行趋势发布，到企业组团赴一线城市参展及每年的国际毛针织服装博览会，都镌刻着这个小镇的产业记忆和城镇变迁。

2016年，中国濮院国际毛针织服装博览会在上海举办。在此次展会上，毛衫时尚小镇进一步扩大了其影响力，吸引了一些优秀互联网公司，为濮院毛衫时尚城市的不断发展带来了创新驱动力，同时还与韩国釜山设计中心签约，直接对接韩国的设计师团队，60位设计师将带来韩国最新流行的设计。

今后三年,濮院镇将总计投资 55 亿元,围绕文化创意、产业集聚等主题,推动一批实打实的项目在濮院落地。从贴牌走向创牌,从制造走向创造,当地政府将把濮院真正建设成为集创意设计、针织材料开发、时装展示发布和旅游驱动为一体的国际一流特色小镇。目前,全镇有 6000 多家毛衫生产企业,从纺纱到染色到生产,有 1 万多家商户、20 余万从业人员,全镇有 3/4 的人口经营着与毛衫关联的行当,濮院居民 90% 的收入来自毛衫及关联产业。未来,濮院毛衫时尚小镇将实现"毛衫之都时装名城"的发展目标,积极向价值链高端迈进!

# Shaoxing

绍 兴

# Yuecheng Rice Wine Town

The Shaoxing Yuecheng Rice Wine Town is located in Dongpu Town, which is famous for producing wine for several thousand years. An old saying goes, "Shaoxing rice wine is well known in the world, in which Dongpu wine ranks among the best." Dongpu, Zhejiang's provincial, historical and cultural town, is the birthplace of Shaoxing Rice Wine. Located in the northwest of Shaoxing City, it is only 8 kilometers away from the city center. Dongpu is the hometown to the great patriotic poet Lu You, who once, with his friends, was boating along Dongpu at night, pleased to sing, "in early spring we visit Dongpu County, smelling the wine scent ten-li away…"

Dongpu has become the most famous wine producing center as early as the Southern Song Dynasty. Song Xiaozong, the emperor, once ordered its "Penglai spring" as the tribute wine. At the time,

Dongpu had assembled a stable of wine shops. The first international gold medal in Shaoxing wine, from the Panama-Pacific International Exposition, had just been won by the Zhouyunji Xinji shop. The shop masters Chen Debao and Xu Jinbao were the industry's influential persons, whose brands of wine were exempt from examination. In that dynasty, Dongpu rice wine had been exported to Beijing, Hong Kong, Southeast Asia and other places.

In 2015, the Shaoxing Dongpu Rice Wine Town was included in the provincial key projects by the provincial development and reform commission. Today, Dongpu Yellow Rice Wine Town is busy building the new Rice Wine Museum of History and Culture, the Rice Wine Hand Workshop, with residential areas and the Rice Wine Experience Street. The construction period is from 2014 to 2017, with a total investment of 5.5 billion, and about 1.24 square meters newly added construction land. In the future, visitors can personally make Zhuangyuanhong or Nüerhong for their sons or daughters which are sealed in the heart of the town; or they can get on a black awning boat, drink rice wine, listen to village theatrical performances, and enjoy the slow life of the millennium town. Rice wine popsicles, rice wine bread, and rice wine mask will also have a great market value among young people.

Dongpu is not only noted for wine, it is also a town of culture and art. It is rich in landscape resources and many historical monuments. There is a state-level cultural relic's protection unit—the former residence of Xu Xilin, a provincial cultural relics protection unit—Recheng Academy, four municipal cultural relics protection units and 4 architectural sites. It retains the civil fire-fighting organization "Shuilong Society," as well as other rare local sceneries such as the Angshang Lake and Silong Bridge. Other 8 high-value historical sites and 45 traditional residential gates preserve many ancient and traditional customs.

Shaoxing Rice Wine is rooted in Dongpu. Dongpu has histories and stories, which become all the elements of rice wine. It will be a characteristic town with brand experience, cultural creativity, and leisure tourism.

# 越城黄酒小镇

越城黄酒小镇位于绍兴东浦镇,有着悠久的酿酒史。俗话说,"越酒行天下,东浦酒最佳"。东浦,位于绍兴市区西北方向,离市中心仅 8 千米,是浙江省级历史文化名镇,是绍兴酒的发祥地。东浦亦是伟大爱国诗人陆游和辛亥革命先烈徐锡麟的故乡。陆游曾与友人从东浦月夜泛舟归大树港,见此处水阔岸长,湖平如镜,明月在天,四野寂然,欣然而歌:"春初访客东浦乡,东浦十里闻酒香……"

东浦,早在南宋就已经是绍兴酿酒行业的中心区域,宋孝宗钦定东浦产的"蓬莱春"为贡酒。当时,这里酒坊云集,绍兴酒的第一枚国际金奖——巴拿马太平洋万国博览会金奖,就是由这里的周云集信记酒坊摘获的。周云集酒坊的酿酒名师陈德宝、徐金宝是当时业界很有影响力的人物,"德意""金宝"牌号的酒成为各地酒行的"免检"产品。在那时,东浦的黄酒已经远销北京、香港、南洋等地。

2015 年,绍兴东浦黄酒特色小镇被浙江省发展和改革委员会列入省级重点建设项目。东浦黄酒小镇将建设新的黄酒历史文化博物馆、观光型黄酒手工作坊、建设特色风情民宿区及黄酒风情体验小街等项目,建设期从2014 年到 2017 年,总投资 55 亿元,新增约 1.24 平方千米建设用地。今后游客来到越城黄酒小镇,可以亲自为儿女酿一坛"状元红"或者"女儿红",封藏于此;或者他们可以乘坐乌篷船,品黄酒,听社戏,享受千年古镇的慢生活。同时,黄酒棒冰、黄酒面包、黄酒面膜等衍生产品也将推向市场,从而扩大消费群体。

东浦不仅是黄酒之乡，也是文化艺术之乡。它有着丰富的景观资源和许多历史古迹，保护区内有国家级文物保护单位徐锡麟故居，省级文物保护单位热诚学堂，4 个市级文物保护点和 4 个建筑遗址。同时，其他 45 处保存较好的传统民居台门和 8 处有较高价值的历史建筑遗址充分展示了当地传统的风土人情。

黄酒的根在东浦，它有历史和故事，有黄酒之所以成为黄酒的一切元素。越城黄酒小镇必将成为具有品牌体验、文化创意和休闲旅游的特色小镇。

# Zhuji Sock-Art Town

In the past thirty years, more than 6000 enterprises and thousands of employees have been Datang's pride to be engaged in sock industries. It was once a legend in the whole world! Today, the area is only 2.87 square kilometers, looking petite, mini, but more lightweight, agile. For more than 30 years of development, The Datang Socks Town has transformed from hand-stocking machines selling small-size goods in baskets to the world's most advanced socks manufacturing center that enjoys the title "International Socks Kingdom."

It has long been a consensus that once a Datang socks machine rings, the world must have a new pair of socks. Only in 2014, Datang produced about 25.8 billion pairs of socks. That means nearly 7 billion people worldwide could get 4 pairs! The reason for the success is not only the Datang's complete, well-developed "industrial chain" consisting of raw materials, machinery production, dyeing and finishing, packaging, marketing, logistics and other whole processes, but also its strong cultural atmosphere. Here, the socks are not just a commodity, but also a bearer of culture, leisure, and tourism. "Datang-made" is not easily copied.

From the appearance, the entire town is similar to a huge "sock," divided into three regions, which are the "Dangtang Silicon Valley," the "fashion market," and the "creative area." When walking into the pavilion of socks town, people will be curious about the socks from the Song Dynasty, Qing Dynasty and the Republican period. Socks-related calligraphy and poetry are also an environment for people's attention to stay. Through the multidimensional images, scenarios and stories, more than 4000 years of the history of Chinese and foreign socks has been exhibited. The ancient and modern socks, with traditional and fashion socks in the exhibition hall are integrated as well.

In the heart of socks town lays a Hosiery think tank. Here the projects are introduced from the Textile Hosiery Institute, Taobao University, the Zhuji Service Center of Tianjin Stock Exchange, the Gaolun New Materials Research and Development Institute, the Hosiery Index Released Center, and other companies. There are 25 universities whose graduate students are regularly settled here to create and research. It has also brought together a number of design talents from famous art institutions, who prefer staying in the town so they can concentrate on creative arts for socks. Chen Renyong, the Chairman of Chuang Mei Cultural Communications Co., Ltd., is one of them. The company he founded is the first successful professional socks product design company. The company now has applied for 8 patents, and has promoted 50 functional sports socks. For example, it produced a kind of ski socks. In a pair of special socks there is a small square bag, in which special heating batteries are placed. With it, you can ensure that athletes will not get frostbite in subzero temperatures.

"The profit of such a pair of sports socks is 500 times higher than that of pair of ordinary socks," Chen Renyong said proudly. It is such young men like Chen Renyong who make the new socks get out from the cocoon like butterflies.

From sports socks to healthy socks, from heated socks to frozen pantyhose socks, from socks for children to fashion socks for adults, various socks show their functions in this town, which all highlights the creative character of "Sock-Art."

# 诸暨袜艺小镇

在过去的 30 多年里，6000 多家企业，数十万从业人员，是诸暨大唐袜业足以傲人的第一基石。而今，这个面积只有约 2.87 平方千米的袜艺小镇，看着娇小、迷你，却更轻盈、矫捷。经过多年的发展，从手摇袜机、提篮小卖到一步步走过来的大唐袜业，在 10 多年前就让美国独霸数十年的"国际袜都"称号成功易主，"世界袜业看大唐"也早已成为共识。

俗话说："大唐袜机响，天下一双袜。"在大唐这个"袜子王国"，仅在 2014 年，就生产了 258 亿双袜子，全球近 70 亿人口差不多每人可分到 4 双！诸暨大唐的袜艺小镇，不仅成为浙江唯一，也是全球唯一的以"袜艺"为主题的特色小镇。大唐袜业能获得这一殊荣，是因为其极为完整、发达的产业链，包括从各种原料、机械的生产，到袜子的生产、染整、定型、包装、营销、物流等全过程；同时，强大的产业基础和浓郁的袜业文化氛围，也是袜艺小镇成功入选的基础。"大唐智造"推动了产业转型升级，实现了产业与文化、旅游、社会的进一步融合，成为大唐袜业无法被轻易复制的一大原因。

从地形看，整个袜艺小镇的外部轮廓，类似一只巨大的袜子，按区域划分又是三只袜子的形状。小镇分别规划了"智造硅谷""时尚市集""众创空间"三大区域。在这里，袜子不只是一件商品，更是文化、休闲、旅游的一个承载体，是"袜艺"与"闲逸"的一次大融合。走进小镇展馆，人们会对宋、清、民国时期的袜子感到好奇，而与袜子相关的书法、诗词，则常让人驻足品味。展馆通过多维形象、情景和故事，将 4000 多年来中外袜子的演变史进行了艺术展现，古老与现代、传统与时尚在这里不断碰撞与融合。

袜业智库是袜艺小镇的心脏，这里引进了纺织袜业研究院、淘宝大学、天津股权交易所诸暨服务中心、高伦新材料研发机构和袜业指数发布中心等单位的相关项目，有 25 所高校的研究生定期入驻进行创作和研究，是人才的创意区和信息的聚合地。在这个创意空间里，还汇聚了一批来自全国各大艺术院校的设计人才，他们在这里专心地进行袜子创艺。80 后的陈仁勇，就是其中的一个，他创办了专注运动袜设计研发的创美文化传播有限公司。自成立至今就已申请了 8 项专利，其中发明专利 3 项，并陆续推出 50 款功能性运动袜。小小袜内有乾坤，前不久，公司完成了一项滑雪袜的设计，这双特别的袜子在脚踝处有个小方袋子，这是专门放置加热电池的。有了它，就可以保证运动员在零下几十度的环境下不被冻伤。一个创意拉升利润成百倍。正是有了像陈仁勇这样的年轻人的"艺"＋"智"，崭新的袜艺小镇才能破茧成蝶。

从运动袜到保健袜，从发热纤维袜到冰冻连裤袜，从儿童学步袜到锦裕时尚袜……这些无不彰显着袜艺小镇的创意本色。

**Jinhua**

金 华

# Yiwu Silk Road Financial Town

Thirty years ago, Yiwu in Zhejiang Province was an unknown poor place, but the smart Yiwu people traveled around to exchange sugar for the wastes from residents in order to obtain low profits. These small businesses gradually started the Yiwu Small Commodity Market, which becomes famous at home and abroad as "Commodity Ocean, Shopper's Paradise" later. Thus, the story of "feathers for sugar" is well-known around the world. In 2011, in the "National Strategy-Comprehensive Reform of International Trade," Yiwu once again was among the trial areas and carried the "Banner of Reform," opening up thousands of new business roads and striving for becoming a national and world-class "International Trade Zone." Today, as the starting point of the new Silk Road, Yiwu has proposed the construction of the "Yiwu Silk Road Financial Town" in China—the Chinese version of "Wall Street" or the Chinese version of "London City."

The Silk Road Financial Town is located in the Yiwu Silk Road New District, with a total planned area of 3.8 square kilometers. In the first two phases, the investment will exceed 70 billion yuan. It will create a regional industrial area reflecting the characteristics of an international trade to speed up the Yiwu financial industry development, to form the specialized, distinctive, and differentiated financial development model, and to enhance the financial services economy, in order to provide the necessary support for comprehensively deepening the reform of international trade. According to Cao Geng, Deputy Director of the Silk Road New District, the Silk Road Financial Town has four main industrial categories: banks, stocks, futures, and insurance. Small loan companies, guarantee companies, trust companies, finance leasing companies and other trade financial institutions are included for the purpose of service market procurement. Public equity (PE), venture capital (VC), and other investment institutions focus on capital operation, international trade in Yiwu.

In the Silk Road Financial Town, what catch the attention of the world most is the soaring skyscraper, which shows the city's ambition and vitality. There is a project locally that the people are quite proud of, the World Trade Center, which is the first city complex in Yiwu, with a total investment of 5.5 billion yuan and a maximum building height of 260 meters. At night, the whole building is lit up glinting with bright stars, emphasizing the magnificent features of the town. "Super high-rise building expresses the ambition of the city, and carries the connotation of culture, like dragons shooting into the sky, which not only highlights this group of buildings' position in the city, but also expresses Yiwu's economy taking off," said the designer of the World Trade Center from the School of Architecture and Urban Planning at Tongji University. In addition to the ultra-high building, there are three 150-meter-high apartment-style hotels, high-end residences, and 148 thousand square meters of commercial podiums which will be a super-large shopping plaza that will completely change the trade imbalance between Yiwu commercial retail and wholesale.

In addition to leading industries, the Silk Road Financial Town blends the multicultural elements in Yiwu with the Jiangnan Cultural Exhibition, in accordance with the provincial government's requirements. As the core business, Yiwu plans international urban functional areas, layouts modern education, medical and international community in order to solve the problems of the theme "Production, City, People" for integrated development. At present, the ecological environment of the Silk Road Financial Town has initially formed. It has built about 667 thousand square meters of the original Ecological Wetland Park to the north of the core area. The next step will be the Yiwu Jiangbin River and Ecological Green Corridor along the river on the south side.

The Financial Town, as a financial pillar of industry, is an important platform for a wealth management center in Zhejiang Province. It is committed to actively creating a favorable environment for the development of industries that attract financial capital and talent gathering and develop financial capital and industrial interaction, which has initially produced an excellent situation.

# 义乌丝路金融小镇

30 年前，义乌在浙江省还是一个鲜为人知的贫困地区，但聪明的义乌人走南闯北，走街串巷，以糖换取居民家中的废物，以获得低收入。从小生意做起，义乌渐渐有了小商品市场，直到成为今天闻名国内外的"小商品的海洋、购物者的天堂"，从而，"鸡毛换糖"的故事也被传为佳话。2011 年，国家战略——国际贸易综合改革试点花落义乌，义乌人又一次扛起改革的旗帜，开辟数千条新的创业道路，争创国家和世界级的"国际商贸特区"。今天，作为新丝绸之路的起点，义乌再次发力，提出建设义乌丝路金融小镇，打造中国版的"华尔街"、中国版的"伦敦城"。

义乌丝路金融小镇位于义乌市丝路新区，总规划面积约 3.8 平方千米，前两期投资将超过 700 亿元。它将形成反映国际贸易特色的区域工业区，加快义乌金融产业发展，形成专业化、差异化的金融发展模式，提升金融服务经济，为全面深化国际贸易改革提供必要支撑。丝路金融小镇主导业态主要有四大类：银行、证券、期货、保险等金融机构，小额贷款公司、担保公司、信托公司、融资租赁企业等以服务市场采购为特色的贸易金融机构，股权投资（PE）、风险投资（VC）等私募基金为代表的专注资本运作的投资机构，国际贸易企业总部和进口贸易企业在义乌的分支机构。

在丝路金融小镇，高耸的摩天大楼显示了城市的雄心和活力，吸引了世界的目光。其中有一个当地人民相当自豪的项目——世贸中心，这是义乌的第一个"城市综合体"，总投资 55 亿元，最高建筑达 260 米。在晚上，整座建筑亮起璀璨的光芒，和夜空的星辰相辉映，充分展现了这座城市的繁华。"超高层建筑表达了城市的雄心，承载着文化的内涵。盛世花开、龙腾义乌的立意，一方面凸显这组建筑物在这个城市中的地位，同时也是表达对义乌经济持续腾飞、繁荣的隐喻。"世贸中心除了超高层建筑外，还有三幢 150 米高的公寓式酒店和高端住宅，以及约 14.8 万平方米超大面积的商业裙房，这将是一个超大的购物广场，将彻底改变义乌商业零售与商业批发的失衡状态。

除了主导产业，丝路金融小镇还根据省政府的要求，在义乌江南岸文化会展功能区融入万国多元文化要素，作为核心区的商务配套。在核心区东北侧，义乌还将规划国际都市功能区，布局现代教育、医疗项目和国际社区，解决"产、城、人"融合发展的问题。目前，丝路金融小镇的生态环境也已初步形成，在核心区北侧已建成约66.7万平方米原生态湿地公园，南侧则是义乌江滨江水系和沿江的生态绿廊。

作为浙江省打造金融支柱产业和建设财富管理中心的重要平台——金融特色小镇致力于积极营造金融行业发展的良好环境，吸引金融资本和人才聚集，金融资本和产业互动发展的良好局面已初步呈现。

# Wuyi Hot Spring Town

Wuyi is the only "China Hot Spring Town" in Zhejiang Province named by the Ministry of Land and Resources. It is about 50 minutes away from Hangzhou by high-speed rail. This small town is like a shining "pearl" along the Jinhua-Lishui-Wenzhou Green Industrial Belt located in the middle of Zhejiang Province. There Guo Dong，Yu Yuan and other ancient villages tell a hundred years of history. Niutou Mountain，Dahong Rocks and other landscapes show the beauty of the canyon，while the natural hot springs offer every kind of rejuvenating treatment and therapy.

The Wuyi hot spring tourism season didn't start early. It did not rise until the end of 1997 with the location of the hot spring only 4 kilometers south of the county. After 20 years of development and construction, the Hot Spring Town gradually became famous in the Yangtze River Delta, and eventually in the country. Now, with characteristics of a small town in Zhejiang Province, the Hot Spring Town has become the new expectations of the Wuyi people. From the spa resort to the ancient residential culture, and from the Fluorite Museum to the development of international comprehensive projects, it shows a picture of quiet and healthy life in the 3.8-square kilometers town blueprint.

Wuyi hot springs yield more than 10000 tons of water in a day, which is rich in minerals. The 42℃-45℃ hot springs transports water from the mouth of the spring to several resort pools. The nearest source of water is undoubtedly in the Chinese Fluorite Museum. With the small but fine features, the 14 bubble pools are all built with jade stones, into which the flow of visitors are restrained daily. In the view of the arts and crafts master Tang Chonggui, it is smaller and more delicate compared to other hot springs. What's more, the ticket prices are relatively low, thus providing high-end enjoyment at low cost. There are also large hot springs to enjoy during the holiday, such as the Qingshuiwan, Qin Hot Spring and the Tang Feng Hot Spring. These complementary advantages are not only reflected on the different hot springs, but also in the interior activities. In the Chinese Fluorite Museum, sculpture learning and the tunnel exploration are great attractions in addition to the hot springs, while in the largest hot spring resort in the Yangtze River Delta, the Qinshui Hot spring

Resort has attracted guest accommodations, dining in Western-style buildings and exotic places. In the summer, it also introduces water parks, the Water-Sprinkling Festival and other entertainments. Similar to the Qinshui springs, the Tang Feng Hot Spring has been taking the classical route with flower arrangement, incense and other health recreational treatments to form a set of hot springs tours.

The Wuyi Hot Spring Town is not just about hot springs. In 2012, the Jing Garden Ancient Dwellings Museum officially started. The ancient dwellings, which had already lost their vitality, were purchased from Jiangsu, Zhejiang and Anhui provinces and then were rebuilt in Wuyi. On New Year's Day 2016, more than 80 ancient houses were re-glowing in the off-site. It is reported that by the end of next year, 36 ancient houses will also be built into high-end hotels, attracting more people to appreciate the charm of traditional Chinese architecture and to create a slow life for the rural track.

The Jing Garden Ancient Residential Museum draws a beautiful color to the hot spring town, but it is not the only highlight. In order to enrich the exquisite form of Wuyi Hot Spring and play out a series of functions of hot spring tours, the local government constructs its new blueprint. In the blueprint, the town is paying attention to what modern urban people aspire to. With an area of about 160 thousand square meters, Xili Bay combines customs, a theme spa, and a vacation village with shopping and entertainment; Fantasy Valley City mixes the modern agriculture with modern science and technology in another area about 2 square kilometers. In the International Car Culture and Experience Garden, 1000 meters of karting entertainment circuit and a standard multi-function track meet the needs of various types of car enthusiasts. In the future, in the surrounding area they will also build a motel, and a Car Camp, combined with the local tour village, tea and other characteristics to create the tourism model of "Sports comes first, and then is relaxation." In the face of such a multi-industry, multi-format, multi-functional spa town blueprint, Zhong Guanhua sincerely visitors can enjoy this healthy, relaxing place.

In October 2016, the International Summit of Hot Spring Town was held in Wuyi. Over 100 guests from Japan, the Netherlands, Singapore, Korea, Taiwan, Hong Kong, and other research institutes, gathered in Wuyi, exploring the spa town development and change. Che Shuobin, Director of the Tourism Management Department of South Korea Soon Chun Hyang University, said Wuyi hot springs was very harmonious, and with the surrounding environment, it was just the right local development advantage. Combined with this advantage, Wuyi Hot Spring Town plans to build a well-known hot spring health resort with health spa, leisure and cultural experience in the world.

Today, Wuyi hot spring tourism has received more than one million visitors with a tourism revenue of more than 2 billion yuan. It provides local people with employment and entrepreneurship, making them become the largest beneficiary group with the income equal to the city's white-collar workers.

# 武义温泉小镇

浙江省武义是国土资源部命名的唯一一个"中国温泉之城",从杭州出发,乘坐高铁 50 分钟左右就可到达。这个位于浙江省中部的小县城就像一颗闪亮的"珍珠"镶嵌在金丽温绿色产业带上。在这里,郭洞、俞源等古村诉说着百年斑驳的时光,牛头山、大红岩等山水景观展现着峭壁峡谷的静美,而天然温泉则更让这里多了份养生的别样韵味。

武义温泉旅游起步并不早。直到 1997 年年底,在县城以南约 4 千米的地方,一个以"温泉"为名的省级旅游度假区才刚开始。经过 20 年的发展和建设,"温泉之城"逐渐闻名于长江三角洲和全国。现在,随着浙江省特色小镇工作的展开,"温泉小镇"的牌子再次成为武义人的期望。从温泉度假村到古老的住宅文化,从萤石博物馆到国际综合项目的开发,在约 3.8 平方千米的小镇蓝图上,一场动静皆宜的养生之旅逐渐有了轮廓。

武义温泉日出水量 1 万吨以上,富含矿物质。水温 42℃—45℃的温泉水,从泉眼分别输向几个温泉度假村的泡池。离泉眼最近的"源头水",莫过于中国萤石博物馆内的温泉体验吧,用"小而精"形容温泉体验吧再贴切不过。14 口泡池,全用翡翠原石、墨玉原石等玉石打造,在省工艺美术大师唐崇贵看来,大而全的温泉度假享受,武义已有清水湾、沁温泉与唐风温泉;温泉体验吧相对其他温泉来说更小更精致,更重要的是,票价相对较低,走的是高端享受、低端消费的路线。这样的优势互补,不仅体现在不同温泉之间,也体现在每家温泉内部。在中国萤石博物馆内,萤石雕刻学习、矿洞探险等体验活动是温泉之外的巨大吸引力。而目前长三角地区最大的温泉度假山庄清水湾、沁温泉，在以西式建筑、异域风情等吸引客源住宿、用餐外，在夏季也推出了水公园、泼水节等娱乐项目。与清水湾、沁温泉相近，一直走古典路线的唐风温泉，用插花、焚香等养生修性内容及与休养团队的全方位对接，形成集温泉、游览在内的全面旅游线路。

武义镇不光有温泉，还有依靠其他文化形成的亮点。璟园古民居博物馆就是其中之一。2012 年璟园古民居博物馆正式动工，一栋栋原本已经失去生气的古民居自江、浙、皖等地收购而来，在武义附建、重塑，到 2016 年元旦试营业，80 余栋古民居都重新在异地焕发了生气。据悉，区域内 36 栋古民居还将打造成为高档民宿，吸引更多人来领略中国传统建筑的魅力，也为游客打造回归农村的慢生活。

璟园古民居博物馆是温泉小镇规划中浓墨重彩的一笔，但也并不是唯一一笔。为了让武义温泉的业态丰富起来，将温泉游的一系列功能发挥出来，当地政府描绘出了武义温泉小镇建设的新蓝图。在这份蓝图里，慢生活、养生这两个现代都市人所向往的内容占了重要位置：占地 16 万平方米的陌上花开溪里湾，融风俗文化、主题温泉、度假、娱乐购物于一体；飞神谷国际慢城，运用国际化的思维，将现代农业、现代科技的一些慢生活理念，融合在 200 万平方米的区域内；而博泉健康养生园，则将温泉康复疗养院搬到了这座以温泉而闻名的小城中，面对这样一张多产业、多业态、多功能并进的温泉小镇蓝图，游客不仅能感受到武义除了温泉以外，也是一个可以养生，可以修心、修身的好地方。

2016 年 10 月，国际温泉小镇峰会在武义举行，超过 100 名来自日本、荷兰、新加坡、韩国、中国香港、中国台湾等研究机构的嘉宾聚集在武义，就温泉小镇发展求变展开探讨。韩国顺天乡大学观光经营系主任车硕彬认为，武义温泉与周边环境非常和谐，这正是当地的发展优势。结合这个优势，武义温泉小镇计划建成以生态为基底、温泉为龙头、养生为核心、产业为主导、文化为灵魂，集温泉养生、休闲度假、文化体验等功能于一体的华东一流、全国知名的温泉度假养生产业集聚区、温泉养生度假旅游目的地。

如今，武义温泉旅游年接待人次已超过 100 万，旅游收入超过 20 亿元。当地群众通过参与就业和创业，也成为最大的受益群体。

# Pan'an Medicinal Herb Town

In the beautiful Pan'an, there is a magical land where people can see the oldest rocks and enjoy the most beautiful "green land" in central Zhejiang. Rare creatures are living in the hidden valleys, and the mountains grow a variety of precious wild medicinal herbs. The time-honored Chinese herbal culture goes forward in this piece of land. Setting foot on Pan'an, people feel like they are walking into a magical kingdom of wild herbs.

Pan'an abounds with Atractylodes, Zhejiang Fritillaria, Scrophulariaceae, and white peony (commonly known as "Pan Five Medicinal Herbs"). Among the world-renowned "Zhejiang Eight Medicinal Herbs", which according to historical records has been planted for more than 1000 years, the prestigious Pan'an Chinese medicinal herbs are highly praised by physicians for their good quality, wide range of applications and good efficacy. Today, Beijing's Tong Ren Tang, Shanghai's Lei Yun, Hangzhou Hu Qing Yu Tang, and other old brand pharmacies are still buying them as a formula medicine.

According to experts' research, Pan'an's good soil conditions, coupled with a complex and diverse micro-ecological environment, are very conducive to the growth of medicinal herbs. The county has 1219 kinds of medicinal plants, accounting for 68% of the herbs produced in Zhejiang province. There are more than 40 kinds of rare medicinal herbs, including Huafu, hawthorn, raspberry, honeysuckle, and wild chrysanthemum. Da Pen Mountain in Pan'an is listed as a national nature reserve, the only one with medicinal plant resources as the main protection. With a large number of rare and endangered medicinal plants and authentic Chinese medicinal plants, Pan'an can be called the unique domestic herbal "gene treasure" which provides a strong resource guarantee for the local production and development of Chinese medicine herbs.

In recent years, Pan'an has extended Chinese herbal medicine's industrial chain. In 2015, Jiangnan Town Construction was included in the county's top ten key projects, and since then the town has strived to integrate Chinese medicinal herb production and marketing with health care, health services, and health products sales to speed up the cultivation of the Chinese Medicine Health Pension Base. Now, Pan'an's Chinese herbal medicine production settles in all the villages throughout the county. More than 80% of its farmers are engaged in the production. The county's planting area is the province's largest Chinese herbal medicine producing area with over 10000 tons of herbal medicine output, whose value is up to 450 million yuan, accounting for approximately 35% of the county's total agricultural value.

Pan'an County, based on the advantages of ecological environment and medicinal resources, actively promotes the standardization of Chinese herbal medicine, which establishes a number of Chinese herbal medicine demonstration bases. One of these bases was Zhejiang Fritillaria standardized demonstration base, which has been listed as the key agricultural standardization project in Zhejiang Province, and another one is the National Agricultural Standardization Demonstration Zone. The Chinese Herbal Medicine Seed Base's construction further strengthens the establishment of the No. 1 Zhejiang Atractylodes, the No. 1 Zhejiang Hu, Zhejiang Shao Sha Seed Base on an approximate 2 square kilometers parcel, which has improved the coverage of Chinese herbal medicine varieties, achieved good economic and social benefits, and played a leading role in the county's traditional Chinese medicine standardization.

A clean and pollution-free ecological environment with a wealth of authentic herbs has attracted many pharmaceutical manufacturers' attention, which has made the land a hotspot for Pan'an enterprises to invest in. For example, Jinling Pharmaceutical has established a Scrophulariaceae GAP base of 2 square kilometers; Lanxi Sanjiang Herbal Pieces Co., Ltd. built a 0. 67 square kilometers Fritillaria GAP base in Xinwo Town. At the same time, brand building has been paid more attention to. In 2011, "Pan'an Five Medicinal Herbs' production and processing technology" was included in the intangible cultural heritage of Zhejiang Province. In 2014, "Zhejiang Eight Medicinal Herbs" were registered as the commodity trademark and 22 service trademarks. Standardization of production has changed the original extensive management. Driven by the leading enterprises, and coupled with the Pan'an County government's support for the industrialization of Chinese medicine, the farmers have changed the concept, and made the production mode of medicinal herbs gradually change from scattered production to contiguous scale operation.

According to reports, Jiangnan Town has an overall planning area of 3.5 square kilometers with a core area of about 1.75 square kilometers, involving Xinwo Town, Shenze Town and the Yunshan Tourism Resort. Its overall layout is "one core, two belts, more bases." Zhejiang eight herbs are the core; Zhuyong expressway and provincial highway are the two economic zones; and the Planting Base for Chinese Herbal Medicine, the Headquarters of the Economic Park, Chinese Herbal Medicine Deep Processing Park, and the Eco-logistics Park, etc., are more bases.

# 磐安江南药镇

位于浙江中部的磐安,有一片神奇的土地!你可以登上最古老的岩石一览最美丽的"绿色",罕见的野生动物隐藏在山谷之中,山间生长着各种珍贵的野生草药,中药材文化在这片土地上传承发扬。走进磐安,人们就像走进了一个神奇的野生药材王国。

世界知名的"浙八味"中就有白术、元胡、浙贝母、玄参、白芍这五味地道药材盛产于磐安(俗称"磐五味")。根据历史记录,"浙八味"已有1000多年的种植历史,磐安中药材由于其质量好、应用范围广及疗效佳而为历代医家所推崇。现如今,北京的同仁堂、上海的雷允上、杭州的胡庆余堂等著名老药店仍在选购"浙八味"作为配方药。

根据专家的研究发现,磐安良好的土壤条件,加上复杂多样的小生态环境,非常有利于草药的生长。全县有药用植物1219种,占全省的68%,有40多种蕴藏量极为丰富的野生药材,包括前胡、山楂、覆盆子、金银花、野菊花等,因而被列为国家级自然保护区,是目前我国唯一以药用植物种植资源为主要保护对象的国家级自然保护区。

近年来,作为"中国药材之乡",磐安不断加强种植中药材产业,拓展产业链。2015年,江南药镇建设又被列入全县十大重点项目,努力整合中药材生产和营销等要素资源,加快培育以保健康疗、养生服务和养生产品销售为特色的中医药养生养老基地。今天的磐安,中药材生产覆盖全县所有村庄,超过80%的农民从事中药材生产。全县中药材产量1万余吨,产值达4.5

亿元,占全县农业总产值的35%左右。

磐安县基于生态环境和药材资源优势,积极推进中药材标准化,建立了一批中药材示范基地,其中浙贝母标准化示范基地被列为浙江省重点农业标准化实施示范项目和国家农业标准化示范区二类项目。中药材良种基地建设进一步加强,建立了浙贝1号、浙胡1号等基地约2平方千米,提高了中药材良种覆盖率。中药材示范基地建设已卓有成效,取得了较好的经济效益和社会效益,对全县中药材的标准化、规范化生产起到良好的示范带动作用。

洁净无污染的生态环境和丰富的地道药材受到许多药品生产企业的关注,磐安成为企业投资建立GAP基地的热土。金陵药业在大盘镇、安文镇、尚湖镇、九和乡等地建立了约2平方千米玄参GAP基地,兰溪三江中药饮片有限公司在新渥镇建立了约0.67平方千米浙贝母GAP基地。同时,该县在品牌建设上也十分注重,2011年"磐五味生产加工技艺"被列入浙江省非物质文化遗产;2014年注册了"浙八味"商品商标、服务商标22个。标准化生产改变了原有的粗放经营,在龙头企业的带动下,加上磐安县政府对中药材产业化的支持,药农的观念逐渐转变,药材生产也逐步从分散生产转向连片规模经营。

据了解,江南药镇总体规划面积约3.5平方千米,总投资103.5亿元。其中核心区规划面积约1.75平方千米,涉及新渥镇、深泽乡和云山旅游度假区部分地区,其总体布局是"一心、二带、多点","一心"就是以浙江浙八味特产市场为核心,"二带"就是诸永高速公路和省道磐缙公路沿线经济带,"多点"就是中药材种植基地、总部经济园、中药材深加工园、生态物流园等。

# Quzhou

衢 州

# Longyou Mahogany Town

On the National Day of 2016 there is such a scene in Mahogany Town, Longyou County: one side is the bustling tourists enjoying the sight; the other side is the workers busy on the construction site. In fact, the Mahogany Town has not opened its gates, but it has attracted a lot of tourists. Only this year, the Mahogany Town has received 2 million people. Why is the Mahogany Town so attractive?

Mahogany is not only an important component of Chinese traditional culture, but also has a very high economic value. Mahogany Town is a cultural industrial project initiated after market research by the Zhejiang Nanaholy Furniture International Group. It plans to cover an area of about 3.5 square kilometers, and invest a total of 8 billion yuan, which will be completed by 2019 after forming productive and ecological areas that are suitable for life. In the future it will become a characteristic town with furniture manufacturing, cultural industries, tourism services, ecological living, and business services. For this reason, the local government issued a series of plans.

Firstly, it provides an industry platform to gather many mahogany manufacturers. Ten years ago, the Zhejiang Nanaholy

Furniture International Group has just settled in Huzhen Town, Longyou County. Under its leadership, Longyou became one of the largest Chinese luxury hardwood furniture research and production bases, and a new mahogany manufacturing center, which provides a better development platform for more mahogany manufacturing. Today's Zhejiang Nanaholy Furniture International Group has developed fast and has made a lead in the domestic counterparts for the 15 successive years, but the Group is not content with the current situation. It began to create a "Mahogany Town" to carry industry development and cultural heritage. After years of brand cultivation and building, the town now has introduced world-class Italian drying equipment, and imported high-quality mahogany from Southeast Asia, Latin America, and Africa. The company's products have been exported to Southeast Asia, Europe, the United States and other regions and countries. In the future planning, the town will be built as the largest mahogany furniture production base, the East China forest trading center, and the Chinese mahogany price index pricing center. Also, it will be established as the largest domestic e-commerce platform, and Asian largest mahogany manufacturing base.

Secondly, it creates a 5A-level scenic spot with its special culture. As previously mentioned, mahogany has always been closely related to traditional Chinese culture. This is why the planning of the town emphasizes the idea of integration, innovation, and Chinese classical culture. In order to give full play to the unique advantages of mahogany culture, the town has built a large number of antique houses. In 2015, the architectural style attracted the attention of film crews. It provided a setting for the film called *Warlord Chi You*, which attracted global attention. In addition, there are many traditional local artisans in the town. Chen Zhenzhong are one of them. Chen's pancake is very unique in the production process, which attracts more tourists to enjoy his cakes.

Thirdly, it customizes a new furniture model. The main consumers of mahogany furniture are usually successful people who are above 40 years old. In order to attract younger customers and broaden the channels of trade, the town is also trying a variety of innovative initiatives to customize their own furniture. As early as in June, 2014, combined with Taobao's "Characteristics of China · Longyou Museum," the town launched personalized high-end services, opened up home manufacturing paths, and also provided space for communication between consumers and designers. It has become a new model of mahogany sales to provide special customized processing to meet the consumers' personal demand.

Mahogany Town is also planning 100 new ecological living buildings，integrating home design with ecological landscape to achieve an energy-saving，sustainable life. Its aim is to create a cultural tourist attraction，while the harmony between man and nature is the most important element of the scenic area.

In accordance with the "Manufacturing Base plus Cultural Tourism" mode，the town is trying hard to build a Chinese mahogany town which integrates arts and culture studies，ecological civilization and health resort.

# 龙游红木小镇

2016年国庆假期,龙游红木小镇呈现出这样一番景象:一边是熙熙攘攘的游客入园观赏,另一边却是工人热火朝天地施工。尽管红木小镇还没有开园,却已经引来不少游客。目前,红木小镇的游客量已超过200万人次。"半成品"的龙游红木小镇为何如此吸引人?

红木,不仅是中国传统文化的重要组成部分,更具有极高的经济价值。也因如此,在2015年首批通过的37个特色小镇中,位于衢州龙游县湖镇镇的红木小镇赫然在榜。龙游红木小镇是由中国年年红家居集团有限公司投资建设的,规划占地面积约3.5平方千米,计划总投资80亿元,到2019年建成后将形成一个集家具制造、文化产业、旅游服务、生态居住、商业服务五大产业为一体的特色小镇。为此,当地政府出台了一系列规划。

首先,小镇提供产业平台,集聚众多红木制造商。10年前,年年红家具集团生产基地才刚刚落户龙游县湖镇镇。而到如今,年年红集团在龙游发展得顺风顺水,并连续15年处于国内同行领先位置,还被誉为红木家居"黄埔军校",仅研发团队就有500余人,产品出口东南亚和欧美等地区和国家。但年年红家具(国际)集团却未安于现状,萌发了打造红木产业发展和将红木作为文化传承新载体的想法,由此,龙游红木小镇应运而生。经过多年的品牌培育和精品打造后,小镇红木制造基地现拥有国际一流的意大利烘干设备,原料全部采用东南亚、拉美、非洲等地进口的优质红木、名贵木材,公司产品出口东南亚及欧美等地区和国家。在未来规划中,小镇将被打造成全国红木家具最大生产基地、华东地区林权交易中心、中国红木价格指数定价中心；打造国内最大的家居产业电子商务平台，并建成亚洲最大的红木生产制造基地。

第二，小镇努力创建5A景区，通过文化体验吸引游客。红木与中国传统文化一直有着紧密的关系。这也是为何在小镇的规划中，着重强调了"创新融合，弘扬国学文化经典"的思想。作为省文化旅游融合试点县，红木小镇在主题确定和文化定位上充分发挥独有的红木文化优势，将国学与红木融合，大量采用红木建造仿古建筑，通过对红木文化的展示、品鉴，融入国学体验、参与等，感受"静心、清心、净心、童心"的心灵成长之乐和智慧修炼之妙；打造达摩文化，增强参观者对源远流长的中国传统文化的认同感和归属感。如此古色古香的小镇建筑风格，吸引了电影摄制组的目光。由纪中传媒集团拍摄的《战神蚩尤》便在此取景，更为小镇拍摄了贴片广告。此外，小镇还有许多传统手艺人的身影。陈振忠便是其中之一。他的"观音素麻饼"的制作工艺独特，吸引了许多慕名而来的游客品尝。

第三，小镇融入文创，体验定制新模式。红木家具的主要消费群体为40岁以上的成功人士，为了能吸引到更年轻的顾客群体，拓宽交易渠道，红木小镇也在尝试各种不同的创新之举。早在2014年6月，小镇结合淘宝网"特色中国·龙游馆"建设，推出红木家私个性化高端定制服务，创新个性化家居制造路径，打通消费者与设计师、制造商之间交流平台，进行特件定制加工，满足消费者红木产品私人定制需求，成为红木销售的新模式。

红木小镇还规划100幢新概念生态居住模式建筑体，融合建筑设计、装修设计、家居设计、生态景观设计等创新设计理念，实现节地、节能、生态可持续的新型居住目标，将家居文化体验充分融入红木文化小镇的整体功能中，打造富有特色的家居文化产业体验区。

按照"制造基地＋文化旅游"模式，小镇正全力打造一个以国学文化为基础，以紫檀文化为背景，融艺术观赏、文化研究、生态游憩、养生度假于一体的中国红木特色小镇。

# Changshan Stone Appreciation Town

From as early as the Northern Song Dynasty, Changshan's unique stones became famous because it was the Emperor Song Huizong's favorite, and Changshan was his must-come place. In the Yongle years of the Ming Dynasty, Changshan's stalagmites were chosen for the Royal Garden of the Imperial Palace which still exists today and has been drawn in Zheng Banqiao's bamboo pictures. In the 1980s, young people from Yan Wushan village, the birthplace of the Stone Town, began to carry stone to markets. In 1997 a market place for trading bluestone and flower stone was set up, which has become the largest professional stone market in East China. There is a place where one can find more than 300 stone business households, with more than 4000 employees. it produces 600 million yuan as an annual output value. It is "China's hometown of stone culture."

However, with the stone industry ever expanding, more and more people feel that the non-renewable stone resources come into increasingly stronger conflict with the enterprises' extensive mining. Industrial transformation lags far behind the market needs. In June, 2015, Zhejiang announced the first 37 provincial-level characteristic towns, which creates a new road for Changshan stone industry—

building the Changshan Stone.Town. The Changshan Stone Town is the first town with stone culture as the theme. The town covers an area of about 3 square kilometers, in accordance with the "one dragon" layout: the tail is the Stone Culture Historic District based on Yan Wushan market; the body is the Stone Culture Corridor along the 048 highway in the north, the head is the Stone Culture Core Area, where the Chinese Stone Culture Park is located; at last the claws are the Stone Processing Park, the Mining Area, and the supporting facilities along the sides.

In addition, the town has a new exploration of the stone financial investment model. In November, 2015, Century Dragon Stone Expo Co., Ltd., and Hong Kong Dagong

Cultural Art Rights Exchange signed a unique stone listing and trade agreement; it also cooperated with Hong Kong Qinianwan Culture and Arts Co., Ltd., to establish the Dragon Enze Cultural Investment Company, to build a leading domestic stone market trading platform. This integration is also reflected in the creation of the new form of stone marketing through the internet. Local government jointed with Alibaba and Tencent to persuade the stone industry men to "take advantage of the internet." Currently, in the Stone Town, there have been six Taobao service stations, and another 11 households to go through the stone network, Alibaba and other platforms, which completed more than 10 million online transactions in 2015.

The integration of industry, culture and tourism in the town will be the new engine to promote local economic, and social development. The stone industry is a huge industry in Changshan, the development of which has benefited thousands of households. This is the biggest highlight, and is the biggest difference from other places.

# 常山赏石小镇

早在北宋时期,常山"巧石"就因深得宋徽宗喜爱而盛名远扬,常山更是其必来之地;明永乐年间,常山石笋石在故宫御花园安家,至今犹存,曾被郑板桥画入竹石图中。20世纪80年代,赏石小镇发源地砚瓦山村的年轻人就开始背着石头闯市场,于1997年成立了青石花石市场,发展至今已成为华东地区最大的青石花石专业市场,现有观赏石经营户300余家,从业人员超过4000人,石产业年产值突破6亿元,是"中国观赏石之乡"。

但随着石产业规模不断扩大,小镇里越来越多的人明显感觉到,石资源的不可再生性和石企业粗放式开采的矛盾日益突出,产业转型升级滞后于市场和消费升级。2015年6月,浙江公布了第一批37个省级创建名单,以常山石产业为基础谋划包装的"赏石小镇"项目名列其中,这给小镇带来了新的发展机遇。为此,常山坚持把文旅基因植入产业发展全过程,并在休闲旅游和环境提升项目上主动融入石元素,把赏石小镇打造成"全域是景区、处处是景观、村村是景点"的新型旅游产业小镇。常山赏石小镇是国内第一个以"赏石文化"为主题的小镇,规划占地约3平方千米,其按照"一条龙"谋划布局,龙尾是以常山石产业起源地——以砚瓦山花石市场为依托的赏石文化历史街区,龙身是沿048省道向北的赏石文化长廊,龙首则是中国观赏石博览园项目所在地——赏石文化核心区,沿线两侧的石材加工园、开采区、配套区为龙爪。

不仅如此,小镇还在观赏石金融化投资模式上有了新的探索。2015年

11月,世纪龙腾石博园有限公司与香港大公文化艺术品产权交易所签订了奇石上市交易协议,并与香港祈年湾文化艺术有限公司合作,成立龙腾恩泽文化投资公司,全力打造主导国内石头上市的交易平台。这种融合还体现在通过互联网开创石头营销新形式上。当地与阿里巴巴和腾讯合作,引导鼓励石产业经营户"触网触电"。目前在赏石小镇区域,已建有6个淘宝服务站,另有11家经营户通过石材网、阿里巴巴等平台销售,2015年完成网上交易额1000多万元。

融合了产业、文化与旅游功能的小镇,将是推动当地经济社会发展的新引擎。石产业是常山的一个庞大产业,特色小镇的建设,让千家万户同步取得效益。这是最大的亮点,也是和其他地方的最大不同。

# Kaihua Root Carving Town

China is famous for root carving in the world, while Kaihua's root carving ranks among the best in China. Zhejiang's Kaihua has a long history of tree-root carving, which can be traced back to the Tang Dynasty. In the fourth year of Tang Gaozu's reign, Du Fuwei took an order to arrest Wang Hua. He built a road through Anhui Province called the "Kaihua Ancient Post Road," which became a big commercial port for the wood business. During the Qing Dynasty, it appeared in a book called the *Kaihua County Records*, which is probably the earliest record of the "Kaihua Tree-Root Carving Art."

However, the person who really carries Kaihua root carving forward and makes it the "Fourth Zhejiang Carving" is a folk art master named Xu Guqing, who is the successor of Xu Root Carving. Over the years, Xu Guqing absorbed the advantages form two different sides. He sustained innovation, and widely enriched the Kaihua root-carving subjects. Thus, he formed the Kaihua Root Carving Artistic Creation Group. In September, 2001, Kaihua County was awarded "China Tree-Root Carving Art Town" by the Chinese Root Artists Association. In 2008, Xu Guqing and Kaihua County government jointly founded the Chinese Root Artists Museum (also known as the Root Palace and Buddhist Cultural Tourism Zone), which plays an important role in the inheritance and protection of the root carving culture. The Chinese Root Artists Museum is a national 5A-level scenic area that covers about 240000 square meters and features the China Root Carving Buddhist Cultural Tourism Zone, the China Root Carving Museum, the Xu Guqing Root Carving Fine Arts Museum, and the China Root Carving Historical Figures Museum. It displays more than 2000 pieces of works related to Buddhist myths, legends, and history, of which the largest single work weighs 40 tons. Therefore, the museum is also called the "World Cultural Heritage" that people have left to future generations.

Today's Kaihua has a blossoming root carving industry. There are a total of more than 30 kinds of root carving enterprises in the county with 2000 employees. It puts out 300000 root carving works in one year, which value at 200 million yuan. Kaihua root carving products are exported to Southeast Asia, Europe and the United States, and has gradually become the province's and even the country's root carving industries' gathering place, forming a China root exhibition.

Kaihua's long history of root carving culture lays a good foundation for creating the Kaihua Root Carving Town. the Kaihua's Root Carving Town, based on its root carving cultural industry, develops Chinese culture, its local industry, and thus forms "Buddhism, learning, ritual, arts, Chan, tea" industries. It promotes eco-industry, financial services, modern logistics, creative design, education, training and other modern service industries. In the next step, it will invite the world art masters and root carving lovers to open production, marketing enterprises, and training institutions, which will make the town the Global Root Carving Cultural Industry Center. In addition, the Kaihua Root Carving Town will focus on the construction of a cultural tourism area, to integrate resources and enhance the industry's overall market competitiveness. It will dig out and cultivate local characteristics, and develop Kaihua paper, Kaihua inkstone, Kaihua porcelain, Kaihua tea, and other traditional industries, producing local style tourism products, to make the root carving industry and the traditional civilized industries into a win-win situation.

# 开化根缘小镇

世界根雕看中国,中国根雕在开化。浙江开化的根雕艺术源远流长,历史可上溯到唐武德四年,杜伏威奉旨降伏徽州汪华,打通了浙西通往安徽的必经之路——开化古驿道。从此开化成为交通枢纽,形成一个以木材经销和水路运输为主的大商埠。清朝光绪年间的《开化县志》记载,大概是开化根雕艺术的最早记录。

而真正将开化根雕发扬光大,并使之成为"浙江第四雕"的则是一位民间艺术大师——徐氏根雕传人徐谷青,他是中国民间一级工艺美术家。徐谷青自幼耳濡目染,爱好雕刻,喜欢绘画,在当地颇有名气。多年来,徐谷青博采众长,推陈出新,广授技艺,丰富根艺题材品种,开拓根艺发展空间,形成了以徐谷青根艺为主的开化根雕艺术创作群。2008 年,徐谷青创办的醉根公司,和开化县政府联合打造了中国根艺美术博览园(又称根宫佛国)。该园的修建在开化根雕的技艺传承与文化保护方面起着重要的作用。中国根艺美术博览园是国家级 5A 景区,占地约24 万平方米,由中国根雕佛国、中国根雕博物馆、徐谷青根艺精品陈列馆、中国根雕历史人物博物馆等组成,陈列着佛儒道、民间神话传奇、历史风云等系列大型根艺作品2000 余件,其中最大单件作品重达 40 吨。博览园堪称世界根雕艺术之都,被誉为今人留给后人、现代留给未来的"世界文化新遗产"。

如今在开化,不起眼的树根已"繁花似锦",结出累累硕果:全县共有各类根雕企业 30 余家,从业人员近2000 名,年产根雕作品 30 万件,产值 2 亿元以上，捧得"中国根雕之乡"称号，百余件根雕作品在省内及全国获奖，根雕产品远销东南亚及欧美国家，已逐步成为全省、全国根雕产业的重要集聚区。

开化根雕历史悠久，并拥有世界上唯一的根雕文化主题公园，为打造根缘小镇创建了非常好的基础。据介绍，开化根缘小镇以根雕文化产业为主导，同时发展国学文化、地方特色文化等产业，形成"佛、学、礼、乐、禅、茶"等产业板块，推动生态产业、金融服务、现代物流、创意设计、教育培训等现代服务业融合发展。下一步小镇计划引进全国乃至世界根艺美术大师、根艺爱好者、根雕生产销售企业、培训机构等，来开化根缘小镇培训、创作、创业，成为全国甚至全球的根雕文化产业中心。除此之外，根缘小镇还将着力于提升根宫佛国文化旅游区，打造以根佛文化为主题的观光游览中心，整合资源，抱团发展，形成规模集聚效应，提升产业的整体市场竞争力，进一步做大开化的生态休闲文化旅游产业；挖掘培育地方特色文化产业，培育发展开化纸、开化砚、开化瓷、开化龙顶茶等传统特色产业，开发生产富有地方风情的旅游产品，使根雕产业和开化传统特色产业在根缘小镇共生共赢。

# Taizhou

台　州

# Huangyan Intelligent Mould Town

Known as "the hometown of Chinese mould," Huangyan has a nearly 60-year history of mould development. The Intelligent mould Town is a specific area in Huangyan with mould industry as the core industry, grafting industrial tourism into local culture tourism features. The total planning area of the town is about 3.5 square kilometers and construction land approximately one square kilometer. The planned investment is about 5.5 billion yuan, from 2015 to 2017, the town will build a high-end mould manufacture center, a small and medium enterprise incubation base, a public service platform, an industrial theme park, and other projects. It strives to become a mould base boasting of domestic leading mould industries with strong international competitiveness, to promote regional, economic, and social development.

Compared with traditional industrial regions, the Huangyan Intelligent Mould Town has the following characteristics: First, using a delicate space-compact model. The town will include mould enterprises, research and development centers, residential flats, supermarkets, banks, theme parks, and others buildings with complete facilities. It is small, but exquisite, just like the Chinese saying, "Small as the sparrow is, it possesses all its internal organs—small but complete." Second, forming complete industrial chains. Mould industries are the leading area in the town, but there are other supporting service industries, such as research and development, as well as information and finance, which can effectively form an innovative industrial chain to achieve the organic integration of resources, speed up the elimination of backward production, and to promote industrial restructuring and upgrading. Third, integrating the industry development and town construction. The planning construction of the town will be combined with the reconstruction of old villages to promote the regional economy but retain the local characteristics and culture, to enhance small town's vitality with a rich spiritual connotation. Fourth, owning the ecologically beautiful environment. The requirements of the town's construction are in accordance with the standards of a 3A-level scenic spots: "ecology is put first, comfortable life second, industrial development last." Through planning the living area, recreation area, commercial support center, and other public service facilities, it aims to build a green beautiful environment with caring and thoughtful service. Fifth, implementing "market-oriented" operation mode. The main part of the town is the enterprises, so giving full play to the market mechanism can stimulate business initiative and creativity, which can inject new vitality into the town's sustainable development.

In addition to the above five features, Huangyan's development can hardly do without its workers. "Moulding is a kind of craft. For our enterprises, we not only need highly educated talents, but also experienced workers who are needed to operate advanced equipment," Liang Bin said, who is chairman of Jingcheng Group. Lin Guogui, one of the "Top Ten Mechanics in the Town," began learning to make mold at the age of 14. For 30 years, he has grown from apprentice to technician to manager, making him highly proficient in the filing, die-casting, grinding, polishing and other techniques. In 2003, Lin Guogui set up his own mold company. With superb technology and unique creativity, his company has become a world-renowned industry giant. At present, his company has cooperated with many famous auto companies, including Mercedes-Benz, BMW, Jaguar, and Land Rover. Although he has been an entrepreneur, Lin Guogui still regards himself as a mechanic. In the company, he does not have his own office, design room, or mold shop. Where he is needed, where his office is. He attributes his success to his own ingenuity. "It is important for mechanics to calm down to delve in things, to polish their own products continuously. That is the spirit of mechanics." Liang Bin said, "it is the most difficult thing to improve precision from 99% to 99.9% in molding. Increasing the accuracy by 0.9% is the core competitiveness of enterprises and will give enterprises hundreds times of profits." In recent years, a significant change is that the mechanics spirit is proposed and increasingly valued. Liu Zhaohui and other front-line workers have become the objects of media coverage and social leaders in new trend, increasingly affecting the community of mechanics in Huangyan. One official in the Huangyan District Organization Department said, "Some activities, such as the election of the town's top ten mechanics, help people to recognize the spirit of the workers and to promote respect for craftsmen and learn from them. Unlike ordinary workers, craftsmen are willing to spend 100 percent of their energy into development and creation of their product, whether it is profitable or not. They regard their products as works of art!" Lin Guogui said, "We need the spirit of the craftsmen to stand out. For an employee and for a business, this spirit is indispensable."

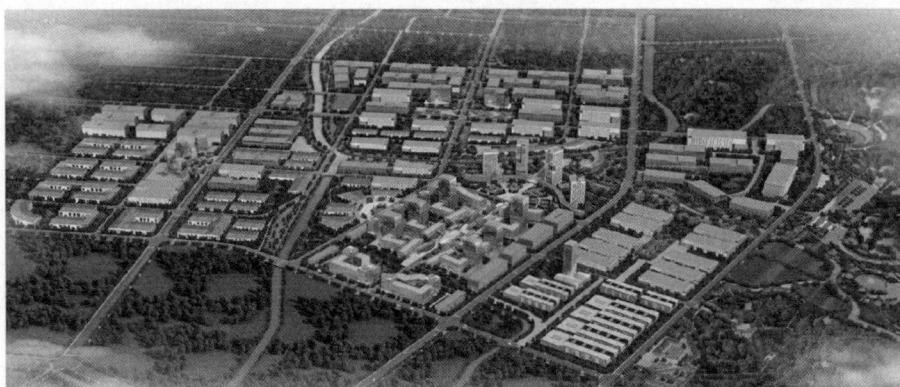

After many years' development, The mould industry Huangyan Mould town has upgraded from low-end manufacturing to high-end industries, from the small lumpy economy to high-tech industrial clusters. By the end of 2014, the region had more than 2000 enterprises with more than 50000 employees, achieving an annual output of 14.5 billion yuan which accounts for one tenth of the total output in China, and with an annual exports value of 300 million dollars. At the same time, it plans to introduce some internationally renowned large-scale mould enterprises from Japan and Taiwan to set up a benchmark for mold industry development. In the near future, Huangyan will grow from China's "mold town" to the world-renowned mold manufacturing base.

# 黄岩智能模具小镇

黄岩素有"中国模具之乡"的美誉，至今已有近 60 年的发展历史。智能模具小镇是一个以模具产业为核心，以项目为载体，嫁接工业旅游及区域特色乡土文化休闲旅游功能的特定区域。小镇规划总面积约 3.5 平方千米，建设用地约 1 平方千米，2015 至 2017 年计划投资 55 亿元，建设项目包括：高端模具智造、中小企业孵化基地、小镇生活商务配套区、模具产业公共服务平台、博览中心及工业主题公园、民俗乡土文化休闲度假村等项目，力争打造成为国内领先的模具产业集聚区和具备较强国际竞争力的模具产业基地，成为带动区域经济社会发展的新增长点。

与传统意义上的产业园区相比，黄岩智能模具小镇具有以下特征。一是空间形态上的"精致紧凑"。小镇范围内将包括模具工业企业、研发中心、民宿、超市、银行、主题公园等多种业态，功能完备、设施齐全，正如"麻雀虽小，五脏俱全"。二是规划布局上的"要素集群"。模具产业是小镇的主导产业，其他配套性服务业，如研发、信息、金融等都要围绕该主导产业进行布局，可以有效集聚技术、人才、资本等多种要素，形成产业链、创新链、人才链、投资链和服务链，实现资源的有机整合和集约共享，促进产业转型升级。三是发展模式上的"产镇融合"。小镇的规划建设将与区域内旧村改造及"美丽乡村"建设相结合，以产业发展及小镇建设带动区域经济社会发展，带动乡土特色文化的挖掘与传播，增强小镇发展活力，丰富精神内涵。四是环境品质上的"生态宜居"。小镇的规划建设要求按照 3A 级以上景区标准进行，坚持"先生态、后生活、再生产"，通过对其中生活居住区、休闲娱乐区、商业配套中心等公共服务设施及景观进行规划建设，营造出一个绿色环保的生态环境、优美舒适的生活环境、贴心周到的服务环境。五是运营方式上的"市场导向"。小镇的建设主体是企业，充分发挥市场机制的调节作用，激发企业的积极性和创造性，为小镇的可持续发展注入新的活力。

除了以上五个特色，黄岩模具小镇的发展离不开长期扎根一线、经验丰富的老师傅。对他们的工匠精神之于企业的重要性，台州精超力模塑有限公司总经理林国贵体会很深。林国贵既是一名企业家，也是一名汽车零件模具设计师。他从 14 岁开始学习制作模具，30 年来，一步步从学徒做到技师再到管理岗位，对锉削、压铸、研磨、抛光等各种工艺，样样精通。2003年，林国贵成立了自己的模具公司，凭借精湛工艺和独特创意，成功牵手多家全球知名的行业巨头。目前，包括奔驰、宝马、捷豹、路虎在内的汽车公司都与他的公司存在合作关系。如今，虽然成了一名企业家，但是林国贵骨子里依然把自己当成一个工匠。在公司，林国贵并没有自己的办公区域，设计室、模具车间，哪里需要，哪里就是他的办公室。他也把自己的成功的原因归结为自己不变的匠心。工匠精神，就是要从 99% 做到 99.9%。这 0.9%的提升，才是企业的核心竞争力，而且会给企业带来百分之几百的利润。近年来，随着工匠精神的提出并日益受到重视，一线工人成了媒体追逐报道的对象，成为社会新风尚的引领者，日渐影响着社会对工匠这个群体的认知。与一般工人不同，工匠愿意花百分之百的精力投入到产品的深度研发与创造中，不论是否盈利，都把它们当成艺术品，不断地精雕细琢。这种工匠精神，正是黄岩模具行业当前所迫切需要的。

经过多年的发展，黄岩模具产业从低端制造向高端智造加速转变，从低、小、散的块状经济向高、精、尖的产业集群不断提升。截至 2014 年底，全区共有模具、配件及相应装备企业2000多家，从业人员 5 万多人，实现年产值 145 亿元,总产量占全国的十分之一,模具年出口量突破 3 亿美元。同时,还计划从日本、中国台湾引入 3 至 5 家国际知名大型模具企业入驻。黄岩区已从我国的"模具之乡"成长为全球知名的模具制造基地。

# Luqiao Volvo Town

As the only automobile industry town in the province's 37 characteristic towns, the Luqiao Volvo Town has attracted phenomenal attention from the beginning. For this reason, the local government seizes the strategic opportunities, and takes the initiative to actively explore ways to promote mutual development of the Volvo Industrial Park and cultural tourism. It focuses on building a model town with industry agglomeration, industrial innovation, and upgrading.

The characteristic town is a new concept, but for Luqiao, it has prepared for a long time to build a very iconic town featuring automobile industry. Luqiao is not only a production and export base for China's economic vehicles and spare parts, but also a production base of national automobiles, motorcycles and accessories. In particular, Geely Automobile returned to the town and set up a Volvo vehicle production base in Luqiao, which rewrites Luqiao's car industry history, provides a good foundation, and is the best opportunity for the Volvo Town's development. In addition, the Volvo Town's location is advantageous. The Taizhou Bay Area where it situates is an important part of the Zhejiang Ocean Economic

Demonstration Zone, and is also the main platform for Taizhou to carry out coastal development and vigorously develop marine economy. Its continuous improvement of roads, hydropower and other infrastructures provides a strong guarantee for the construction of the Volvo Town.

The Volvo Town is located in the core area of Pengjie Town, Luqiao District and Taizhou Bay Circular Economy Industrial Park. According to the plan, the Luqiao Volvo Town has a total area of about 6 square kilometers. With Geely V car project as the core, it has three major characteristics: the automotive industry, automotive culture and car tourism. It also aims to develop automotive vehicles parts, creative product design, car theme tourism, e-commerce and other industries. The town's development follows the principle of "one planning, distributed implementation, persistent development" and adheres to the industrialization and urbanization interaction. Its goal is to build a nationally advanced volvo automobile production and research base, and an eastern China auto parts production base and trade center. At the same time, it will build into the Coastal Tourism and Leisure Base a livable auto-themed new area.

The whole construction period of the town is from 2014 to 2020. After its completion, it will produce 0.2 million Volvo cars every year. With about 3 million residents and workers, reaching 100 billion yuan as an output value，and realizing more than 4. 5 billion in tax revenues. It will attract more than 250000 people each year. Combined car elements with the Nordic elements—the original form of Volvo，Luqiao will be an amazing area with car industries.

# 路桥沃尔沃小镇

作为全省第一批 37 个省级特色小镇创建名单中唯一一个汽车工业小镇，沃尔沃小镇从规划开始，就受到了无数关注。为此，当地政府也抢抓战略机遇、谋势而动、主动作为，积极探索推进沃尔沃产业园区与城市开发、现代商贸、文化旅游的一体化、融合式发展，着力打造产业集聚、产业创新和产业升级的样板小镇。

特色小镇是一个新概念，但是对于路桥来说，打造一个极具标志性的汽车小镇却准备已久。路桥不仅是中国经济型汽车及零部件生产出口基地，也是全国重要的汽车、摩托车及配件的生产基地。特别是吉利控股集团的回归——吉利汽车将在路桥设立一个沃尔沃的整车生产基地，它的建成投产将重新书写路桥的汽车产业历史，并为打造沃尔沃小镇提供良好的基础和最好的发展契机。除此之外，沃尔沃小镇位置得天独厚，台州湾集聚区是浙江海洋经济示范区的重要组成部分，也是台州实施沿海开发、大力发展海洋经济的主要平台。台州湾集聚区道路、水电等基础设施不断完善，为小镇建设提供了强有力的保障。

沃尔沃小镇位于路桥区蓬街镇和台州湾循环经济产业集聚区核心区域，规划面积约 6.09 平方千米，主要分为三大功能区：一是吉利沃尔沃整车生产基地；二是汽车零部件产业基地，涵盖零部件产业园区、物流园区、办公研发区等；三是体现北欧风情的生活区，涵盖吉利 V 项目生活配套区、汽车主题公园、北欧风情街、汽车创意产业园、休闲娱乐区、滨海绿带等。小镇开发遵循"一次规划、分步实施、滚动发展"的原则，坚持工业化、城镇化互动，目标是建设成为全国先进的沃尔沃汽车生产和研发基地及中国东部重要的汽车零部件生产基地、贸易中心，同时建设以汽车为主题的滨海旅游休闲基地和宜居的城市新区。

小镇建设周期为 2014 年至 2020 年，整个建成后将形成年产 20 万辆沃尔沃汽车的产业特色小镇，集聚人口约为 3 万人，年产值将达1000亿元，实现税收 45 亿元以上，每年吸引各地旅游人数 25 万人次以上。路桥沃尔沃小镇将把汽车元素和北欧元素完美结合，必将成为一个以汽车产业为特色支撑的示范小镇。

# Xianju Natural Oxygen Bar Town

An ancient Chinese saying expression is "Any mountain can be famous with the presence of an immortal, even if it's not very high; and any river can be holy with the presence of a dragon, even if it's not very deep." These words are just what the Xianju Oxygen Bar Town well deserves. The Xianju Oxygen Bar Town is located in the middle of Baita town in Xianju County, with a total area of approximately 5 square kilometers. In recent years, with the development of the scenic areas, it has become well-known for the natural scenery. With the supplement of the Great Health concept, it gradually became a new model for the "Green Rise."

"Green" is the most outstanding characteristic in the Xianju Oxygen Bar town, and it also illustrates the superiority of the local natural environment. From a long distance, the tall gate of the Xianju Oxygen Bar Town is like a picture frame, with the background being odd mountains, different waters, and floating clouds, which is also sketched into a long scroll of a natural ink painting. In the long pavilion surrounded with clear water, trees and flowers are breathing in the mist, fountains are elegantly jumping on the lake with musical rhythm, all of which reminding people of a wonderland. Now, the Oxygen Bar Town has been promoting a project—the Shenxianju SPA Health Base. The project will be composed of the SPA Beauty, Preservation & Longevity Base with theme resort hotels, a commercial plaza, and real estate parcels. It's planning 5 major health zones and 8 beauty regimens. Investors have completed the project and construction design.

There also lies a famous village full of "immortal air" called the "Big Dipper Village," whose real name is Gaoqian Village, and is the settlement of a prominent family known as "Wu" from the southern region of the

Yangtze River. According to legend, during the Ming Dynasty, the Wu brothers had the same dream one night. In the dream, the celestial skies showed the south of Gaoqian Village, where seven stars surrounded the moon and the "Dragon Root" was strong in the background, which means this was a treasured place to produce good harvests. So the brothers built their house there, which was later expanded by their sons. In the Xianfeng years of the Qing dynasty, it grew to be 13 large-scale buildings. As time went by, Gaoqian Village remained well preserved, except two ancient houses were burned during the period of the Republic of China, the rest stayed well preserved. There are eight houses that are currently open to the public. In the village, these buildings make people feel like they are in a sculpture museum in the southern of the region Yangtze River. The wood carvings on the pillars are rich and noble, the stone carvings exquisite and atmospheric, and window lattice carvings and brick carvings are amazing.

It not only is a vast area, but also is a remarkable place that portrays outstanding personalities. The village has produced public officials for several generations. Gaoqian Village is also the birthplace of Xianju lanterns, which represent a profound cultural and artistic achievement, and are the crystallization of hard-work and wise people. The Xianju lantern is currently included in the country's first batch of non-material cultural heritage items, and has been printed on Chinese stamps. Included in Chinese history and culture, the ancient village is listed as a historical and cultural protected area in Zhejiang Province.

The Xianju Natural Oxygen Bar Town is a crucial part in Xianju's "Green Rising." After the completion of this town, it will become the platform for xianju's tourism and a major carrier of expanding effective investment and promoting the project construction.

# 仙居神仙氧吧小镇

古人云："山不在高,有仙则名。水不在深,有龙则灵。"这话对于仙居神仙氧吧小镇可谓当之无愧。神仙氧吧小镇位于仙居中部的白塔镇,总面积约5平方千米。近年来,随着大神仙居景区的开发,这个以自然风光见长的旅游胜地声名鹊起,再辅以"大健康"的理念,正逐渐成为"绿色崛起"的新样板。

"绿色"是仙居氧吧小镇最大的卖点,这也正说明当地自然环境的优越。入眼是高耸的门庭,犹如画框;背景是奇山异水流云,勾勒成一幅天然水墨长卷。漫步在长亭碧水间,山水、树林、花草在薄雾里呼吸,优雅的喷泉随着音乐在湖面上律动,一切恍若仙境……在仙居氧吧小镇,一幅人工和自然融合的山水长卷,令天南地北的游客流连忘返。这里生态良好,植被覆盖率高,水域面积广,负氧离子浓度奇高。据测算,平均每立方厘米负氧离子含量为2万至3万个,最高一处测得8.8万多个,超出了仪器的峰值,这也正是"氧吧小镇"的由来。如今,氧吧小镇已在推进"神仙居SPA养生度假基地"项目。由SPA美容养生基地、特色主题度假酒店、商业广场、景观房产组成,规划五大养生区和八种美容养生模式。

小镇还有一个充满"仙气"的村落——"北斗七星村",真名叫高迁村,是江南望族吴氏的聚居地之一。相传明朝末年,仙居白塔镇吴氏族人兄弟做了相同的梦:仙人指点高迁村南面,天上七星环月,地下龙脉健旺,是五谷丰登、人才辈出的风水宝地。于是兄弟俩在这里树屋造宅。经过子孙们的扩建，至清朝咸丰年间，建成了规模宏大的六叶马头四开檐楼房十三座。随着时间的推移，除了民国时期因失火被烧毁的两座，其余都完好保存，有八个宅院对外开放。走进高迁村，仿佛置身于一个"江南雕刻博物馆"。古宅梁柱上的木雕浑厚而尊贵，石雕精致而大气，窗棂木雕和砖雕艺术更让人叹为观止。古人云"人杰地灵"，而高迁古村恰恰培养出了不少人才。这里古代多出官宦人家、进士、举人，现代也出了很多有名望的人士。高迁古村是仙居花灯发源地之一，花灯艺术蕴涵了深厚的文化艺术内涵，是当地人民勤劳智慧的结晶，目前仙居花灯被列入国家第一批非物质文化遗产。在历史文化的积淀和灌溉下，高迁古村也被列为浙江省历史文化保护区。

仙居氧吧小镇是仙居"绿色崛起"的关键一环，建成之后这个小镇将成为仙居旅游转型升级的平台，从原来单纯的观光旅游转向观光与休闲度假相融合，同时也将成为扩大有效投资、推进项目建设的一个主要载体和抓手。

**Lishui**

丽　水

# Liandu Ancient Weir and Painting Town

It is known that on March 22, 2015, the Lishui Ancient Weir Project was inscribed on the World Heritage List by the China National Irrigation and Drainage Committee; only one day later, the Painting Town stood out as one of the first 28 characteristic towns of Zhejiang Province. Recently, the Ancient Weir and Painting Town has attracted a lot of tourists with its unique charm.

The Ancient Weir and Painting Town has a long history and rich heritage. A total of 10 camphor trees with more than 1000 years of age are planted on the river banks. Such millennial camphor trees are rarely seen in the country. They have deep roots in the weir embankment, firmly guarding the town, and also witnessing the long history of ancient weir. In the center of the town square there is a towering camphor tree, which is the largest one with a 1500-year history. It spans an area of more than 500 square meters, and its trunk is up to 7.45 meters, which is so huge that six adults could barely hold it together. These ancient camphor trees are also regarded as Feng Shui trees and tree gods. There exists a custom from "Five Elements Theory" that goes like this: If a newborn is in lack of wood, he will be held before the camphor tree and recognizes the camphor tree as a godparent, the tree will protect him growing up peacefully and healthily.

The Ancient Weir and Painting Town has China's unique Lishui Barbizon School of Painting which attracts artists painting on the riverside. Barbizon is a small beautiful village located about 50 kilometers from the south of Paris. Around 1850, it was a remote village with no church, no post office, no school, but only two of the shops that were filled with painters who were fascinated by its landscapes and simple folkways. After Rousseau moved here from Paris, a large number of artists such as Corot and Mille followed to live here. It became a "Painters' village," later known as the "Barbizon School" in the history of painting. Although the Ancient Weir and Painting Town is a long distance from Barbican, France, they have a common feature—the beautiful scenery. Lishui painting groups are inspired by the French Barbizon School, and based on the town's pretty hills and shores as material. Their works not only embodies the characteristics of a realistic school, but also contain the modernist's creative techniques. After years of practice, the works achieved good results in a variety of exhibitions and gradually formed a school of art. Distinguishing from the French Barbizon School, it is called the Lishui Barbizon School.

Ancient Weir and Painting Town is also well-known for Oujiang River which has more than 100 species of fish. The town is the cultural display of the Lishui Kowloon National Wetland Park and is the important block of the Oujiang River Tourism Resort. With the waters of more than 92%, the scenic area is graded as Class II in "National Water Quality Standard" and Class I in "Air Quality." The Ecological Vegetation is based on native beach forest, thatch, and reeds. In autumn, there are acres of straws along the river with kernels sending forth a certain aroma, which looks attractive. This good ecological environment is the habitat of good egrets. There are many egrets: large egrets, small egrets, yellow-eared egrets, and so on. In the town river live hundreds of wild freshwater fish, which the local residents used to refer as Stream Fish. The species includes spinibarbus caldwelli, mandarin fish, grouper, pelteobagrus fulvidraco, and so on. People who come here all like tasting them, which has become the specialty of the town.

Now the Ancient Weir and Painting Town has become a special town featuring tourism and a painting industry which promotes economic development. According to the statistics, the income of local farmers increased by nine times from 2005 to 2014. More than 800 people are directly engaged in the work of the local tourism services. The painting industry, which is the main industry, highlights the cultural characteristics of the ancient town. In the future the town will establish an oil painting base, an oil painting exhibition base, an oil painting trading base and an oil painting sketch base. In the near future, the Ancient Weir and Painting Town is aiming at becoming a national 5A-level scenic spot, with plans to construct a livable, suitable and interesting place.

# 莲都古堰画乡小镇

2015 年 3 月 22 日，在中国国家灌排委员会工作会议上，丽水通济堰水利灌溉工程被授牌列入首批世界灌溉工程遗产名录；而仅仅隔了一天，在 3 月 23 日的全省服务业特色小镇评审会上也传来了捷报，古堰画乡特色小镇脱颖而出。如今，这个独具魅力的古堰画乡小镇吸引了许多游客的到来。

古堰画乡有着悠久的历史，现存古樟树一共 10 棵，树龄都在 1000 年以上，如此规模的千年古樟树群在国内都是罕见的。古樟树分布在主干渠两岸，树根深扎堰堤，牢牢地护卫着堤岸，也见证了古堰的变迁。特别是广场中心的一棵参天古樟，它是大港头渡口老香樟树中最大的一株，已经有 1500 多年的历史，树冠覆盖面积超过 500 平方米，主干达 7.45 米，需要 6 个大人才能合抱。这些古樟树还被当地人视为风水树和树神。当地有个风俗，小孩出生后五行缺木，都会被抱到樟树前，举行一个朝拜仪式，认樟树为干娘，以保佑小孩能平平安安长大，像樟树这样长命百岁。

古堰画乡独特的"丽水巴比松画派"，吸引着大师们到江边写生。巴比松是巴黎南郊约 50 千米处的一个风景优美的小村落。1850 年前后，它还是一个偏僻的小村，但它仅有的两家客店却住满了来这里写生的画家，这里迷人的风景和淳朴的民风吸引了他们。先是卢梭从巴黎迁居于此，接着柯罗、米勒等大批画家也到这里居住，巴比松几乎成了"画家村"，画史上的"巴比松画派"便由此开始。法国巴比松虽然和古堰画乡相隔很远，但是它们都有一个共同的特点——优美的风景。丽水油画群体受到法国巴比松画派的启迪，借鉴法国巴比松画家的精神：画我家乡，走向自然。他们扎根丽水，以秀山丽水为素材，作品既体现了现实主义流派的特征，又蕴含着现代主义的创作手法。经过多年的实践，所创作的作品在各种展览中取得了好成绩，在省内外产生了一定的影响，逐渐形成了一个艺术流派，与法国巴比松画派异曲同工，由此外界称丽水油画艺术为"丽水巴比松画派"。

小镇瓯江溪鱼也远近闻名，野生淡水鱼种类多达百种。古堰画乡景区是丽水九龙国家湿地公园的文化展示区和瓯江省级旅游度假区的重要组成区块，92%以上的河段为国家 II 类水质标准，空气质量 I 类标准；生态植被以原生的滩林、茅草、芦苇为主，金秋时节，景区沿江近千亩的茅杆群，茅穗飘花，别有一番情趣。良好的生态环境是白鹭栖息繁衍佳地，这里的白鹭品质众多，有大白鹭、中白鹭、小白鹭、黄嘴白鹭等。古堰画乡的各河段是华东地区溪流性鱼类的集中地，野生淡水鱼种类多达百种，当地人习惯统称为"溪鱼"。特色品种有：厥旦、刺鲃、鳜鱼、厚唇鱼和石斑鱼等。瓯江溪鱼，是大港头镇和碧湖镇地方特色菜系的招牌菜，食之回味无穷，是难得的美味佳肴。

古堰画乡作为旅游产业类特色小镇，主要产业包括旅游业和画产业。据不完全统计，2005 年到 2014 年，景区核心村农民人均收入增加 10 倍，当地直接从事旅游等服务业的人员超过 800 人。而画产业是突出古堰画乡文化特色的另一主要产业，现建有丽水巴比松陈列馆、丽水油画院、古堰画乡展览馆、古堰画乡分校等。未来小镇将主要打造油画创业基地、油画展示展览基地、油画交易基地和油画写生基地，并将举起"中国写生基地"这块大旗。目前，古堰画乡景区正围绕国家 5A 级景区建设目标，着力谋划建设"宜居、宜业、宜游、宜文"的古堰画乡风情小镇。

# Longquan Celadon Town

China has five famous kilns, among which the Ge kiln refers to the Longquan Celadon. According to research, the Longquan Celadon has a 1700-year history. Because of its fine porcelain, which has a green and crystal color, bright and smooth lines, and dignified modeling, Longquan has been well-known and is at the top of the porcelain world. However, in 1465, the Ming Dynasty implemented the Sea Prohibition. Since then, the Longquan Celadon began to decline. During the twenties and thirties of the last century, the Longquan almost became a barren hill, leaving only debris. In 1957, Premier Zhou Enlai clearly pointed out the necessity of restoring the production of the five major historical kilns, especially the priority of the restoration of Longquan kiln. Therefore, the Longquan Celadon began to resume production. After 50 years of efforts, the Longquan Celadon has risen to fame and regained its former glory.

The core area of the Celadon Town is located in Shangyang Town, in the western part of Longquan City. It is 36 kilometers away from the urban area. There the natural landscape is fabulous, the porcelain clay is rich, and the folk porcelain making is flourishing. Shangyang, as the birthplace of modern Longquan celadon, has witnessed the development of modern Longquan celadon's history. In the town of Shangyang, porcelain charms are overflowing on the streets and lanes. The previous state-owned porcelain factory offices, celadon institutes, large chimneys, and dragon kilns still exists, and has become a period of celadon cultural history that cannot be copied.

In 2015, the Longquan Celadon Town was included in the first 37 characteristic towns in Zhejiang Province, which made the traditional industry get a new opportunity for development once again. At the end of 2015, the Longquan municipal government successfully signed a cooperative agreement with the Shanghai Daoming Company on the China Celadon Town Development Project. Under the agreement, the Shanghai Daoming Company will invest about 3 billion yuan to build the China's Celadon Town in 5 years. The construction projects include two areas: Shanghai and Longquan. Among them, the Longquan Celadon Town covers a land area of about 467 thousand square meters, including the Piyun Celadon Culture Park, a 1957 creative design base, the International Ceramic Village, the International Ceramics Exhibition Center, the Tourism and Leisure Center, the Celadon Research and Development, and the Industrial Agglomeration Development Base; while in Shanghai there will be about 4000 square meters for the Celadon Exhibition Center. As a consequence, the China Celadon Town will have an international exchange platform to promote research and development creativity in Shanghai. In the meantime, there exists a characteristic town in Longquan that

disinters the historic classics, focuses on cultural creativity, and owns unique cultural connotation and leisure features.

The construction of China's Celadon Town will open an international door to the Longquan Celadon Town. After the completion, the annual number of tourists is estimated to be up to 0. 3 million, with the celadon industry achieving annually a 1 billion yuan output value and providing 1000 jobs directly. Changing more Longquan people's life by celadon will no longer be a dream.

# 龙泉青瓷小镇

中国有五大名窑，其中的哥窑，指的就是龙泉青瓷。据考证，龙泉青瓷迄今已有 1700 多年的历史，以瓷质细腻、色泽青翠晶莹、线条明快流畅、造型端庄浑朴著称于世，曾长期问鼎世界瓷器之巅。然而在 1465 年，明朝实行了海禁，"片板不许下海"，自此，龙泉窑开始日薄西山。到 20 世纪初，龙泉的青瓷窑火几乎完全熄灭，到 20 世纪 20—30 年代，大窑群干脆成了一片荒丘，只留下遍地碎片。1957 年，周恩来总理明确指示要恢复全国五大历史名窑的生产，强调要优先恢复龙泉窑和汝窑的生产。龙泉青瓷开始恢复生产，经过 50 多年的努力，龙泉青瓷再度声名鹊起，重铸昔日辉煌。

龙泉青瓷小镇核心区位于上垟镇，地处浙闽边境龙泉市西部，距市区约 36 千米，山水资源优越、瓷土资源丰富、民间制瓷盛行，历百年不衰。上垟镇作为现代龙泉青瓷发祥地，见证着现代龙泉青瓷发展的历史。走进上垟镇，深山小镇的瓷风古韵从翻新的大街小巷里飘溢出来，曾经的上垟国营瓷厂办公大楼、青瓷研究所、大烟囱、龙窑、倒焰窑等至今仍在，成为不可复制的青瓷文化历史。

2015 年，龙泉上垟青瓷小镇列入首批浙江省 37 个特色小镇创建名单，传统产业遇到了新机遇，当年年底，龙泉市政府就与上海道铭公司成功签订了中国青瓷小镇开发项目合作协议。根据协议，上海道铭公司投资约 30 亿元人民币，以 5 年为建设周期，全力打造中国青瓷小镇。该建设项目包括上海和龙泉两大区域。其中，龙泉上垟青瓷小镇的项目用地面积约 46.7 万平方米,包括披云青瓷文化园、1957创意设计基地、国际陶艺村、国际陶瓷会展中心、旅游休闲度假中心、青瓷研发和产业集聚发展基地等项目,在上海则将建设约4000平方米的青瓷展示中心。届时,中国青瓷小镇项目将在上海拥有研发创意、宣传展示国际化交流平台,在龙泉拥有重现历史经典、聚焦文化创意、具有独特文化内涵和休闲度假功能的特色小镇。

中国青瓷小镇的构建,将为龙泉青瓷工业打开一扇国际化的大门。小镇落成后,年旅游人数可达30万人次以上,青瓷工业将实现10亿元年产值,可直接提供就业岗位1000个。让青瓷改变更多龙泉人的生活,将不再是梦想。

# Qingtian Stone Carving Town

Qingtian stone is one of "China's Four Famous Stones." It is the ancient stone carving experts' preference for its clear and light color. For example, the top-grade Qiantian stone, "Fengmenqing," is known as the "Stone Gentleman," because of its rarity, elegant color, gentle quality, and moderation, just like the modest and refined scholars. Qingtian stone carving is also well-known for hollow engraving techniques which are combined spirit with shape, complete without losing the exquisite. It's really amazing.

Qingtian stone has a long history, which can be traced back to "Song Ze culture" about 6000 years ago. With tone cut and one chisel, stone carving artists designed them according to the characteristics of stones. Due to using material and colors according to art demand, Qingtian stone got "embroidery on the stone" reputation. Qingtian stone was once the material for older generation who made the world know about Qingtian. Through the "exquisite treasure," some foreigners began to understand the place. Since 2006, Qingtian county government has proposed strategic objectives of building a town for "China Stone Culture," to develop and strengthen the stone culture industries. Since then, a series of policies have been introduced to promote the stone industries in the county. Up to now, the stone-based projects have been under construction, which include the Stone Carving Industrial Park, China's Stone City, a stone carving handicraft market and the Qingtian Stone Museum. At the same time, Qingtian's Stone Arts Museum and the Chinese Original Stone Market are being planned to initially realize integration of stone carving, touring, and selling, and will gradually become the largest distribution center in China.

In 2010, in order to further expand the culture tourism, Qingtian strung several attractions into a chain, which created the first 4A-level Stone Tourist Route. With the new cultural concept, it achieved the mutual development of stone culture and tourism. A visitor from Wenzhou, said, "In the past, if we wanted to appreciate Qingtian stone culture, the only way was to go to a business or household. Later, we could go to the stone city. But now in Qingtian, we enjoy the beauty of rock stone culture at a theme park, while viewing the Qingtian stone culture and history, which is really exciting!"

Although Qingtian stone is famous at home and abroad, it has always been labeled as expensive for ordinary people to afford. In recent years, the Qingtian government, by the means of a stone flea market and Internet technology, has begun to meet the needs of ordinary people, hoping to put these "noble" products into the homes of ordinary people. In addition, the development of the stone industry is gradually undergoing the transformation and upgrading from the workshop-style production to industrial transformation. Therefore, the town has organized a Stone carving Complex and Da'an Stone Carving Creative Park, which brings retail investors together to achieve integration of processing, marketing and exhibiting. The combination of traditional, hand-made stone with 3D printing, internet, and other modern technologies also helps to realize the characteristic town's transformation. For example, Zhang Xufeng, who was born after 1980, opened an online shop featuring Stone Carving Practice Seals. The turnover for the past two years of his shop has more than 3 million, of which 80% are from online. Last year, on "Double 11" Shopping Festival he got tens of thousands of online seal orders. In Zhang Xufeng's view, Qingtian stone, in the past, has stayed on the list of expensive products, making varieties of stone products not rich enough. According to his words, exploring small stone carving products is very important, which will provide a great space for development.

In today's Qingtian, there are more than 20000 stone carving practitioners, and the stone carving industry has an annual output more than 400 million yuan. They began to make "beautiful stone" sing a new song to tell the world about another stone culture legend.

# 青田石雕小镇

 

    青田石作为"中国四大名石"之一，色泽尚清、尚淡，是历代篆刻家首选石料，青山石中的上品——封门青因数量奇少，色泽高雅，与文人雅士含蓄而不张扬的品质相契合，被誉为"石中君子"。青田石雕以镂雕技艺见长，精雕细刻，神形兼备，大气之中不失精妙，令人叹为观止。

    青田石雕历史源远流长，最早可追溯至6000年前的"菘泽文化"时期。凭借着一刀一凿，石雕艺人根据石材的特点展开构思，因材施艺，依色取俏，有在"在石头上绣花"之美誉。青田石曾经是老一辈青田人走向世界让世人认识青田的物证，许多外国人正是通过"精美的石头"了解物华天宝的青田。自2006年以来，青田县委县政府提出打造"中国石文化之都"的战略目标，大力发展、壮大石文化产业。自此，一项项政策、举措纷纷出台，推动着该县的石雕产业快步向前迈进，中国石雕城、中国石雕工艺品市场、青田石雕博物馆等项目的陆续建设，有效提升了产业层次。同时，又规划兴建青田石雕大师艺术群馆和中国原石市场，初步实现石雕"产、赏、销"一体化，成为国内最大的名石集散中心。

    为进一步做大石文化旅游，2010年，青田县还将石雕博物馆、千丝岩石文化公园和中国石雕城等景点串珠成链，精心创建了国内首条石文化4A级旅游线路，以全新的石文化理念，实现石雕文化与旅游的"比翼双飞"。一位来自温州的游客说："过去，慕名来青田领略石雕文化，只有到经营户家中去看，后来可以去石雕城看，现在来青田，还可以在千丝岩的石文化主题公园里一边欣赏美景，一边纵览青田石雕的文化和历史，真可谓美不胜收！"

虽然青山石雕名扬海内外，但一直以来，石雕都被贴着"高大上"的标签，曲高和寡，普通百姓难以拥有。近几年，小镇通过石雕跳蚤市场、互联网技术等手段，不断满足普通群众的需求，希望让这些"高贵"的产品走入寻常百姓家。但石雕产业的发展最终还是要走转型升级的路子，由作坊式生产向产业化生产转型。为此，当地政府规划了石雕综合体、大安石雕创意园等，将散户集中起来，实现加工、销售、展示一体化，并坚持把石雕产业发展、石雕华侨文化挖掘和旅游观光建设融合发展，把传统手工制作和3D打印、互联网、物联网等现代技术相结合，在产业转型升级中助力特色小镇建设。80后的张旭峰就是率先尝到甜头的一位幸运儿。他的网店主打产品是石雕练习印章，客户群体锁定在学生和退休干部中。"这两年的营业额都有300多万元，其中80%的销量来自线上，去年'双11'当天收到了上万枚印章的网上订单。"在张旭峰看来，以往青田石雕产品多停留在创作生产价位较高的艺术品、收藏品和礼品上，使得石雕产品创作品种不够丰富。按他的话说，"打破单一的产品模式，比如深度开发一些石雕新工艺小产品，会有巨大的发展空间"。

今天的青田，有2万余石雕从业人员，石雕产业年产值达4亿多元。他们开始让"精美的石头"唱起新歌，向世人述说着"美石美刻"的精彩及"石文化之都"的传奇。

# Jingning She Group Town

---

As early as 766 A. D. , an ethnic group named "She" migrated from Fujian to Jingning, Zhejiang. Over the past 1000 years, dozens of She villages scattered among the Jingning fields, making Jingning the only She Autonomous County in China. In June, 2015, She Town in Jingning County was announced as on the first list of provincial-level towns known for tourism development. With government support, She Town is planned to cover an area of 3. 9 square kilometers. With the construction area of one square kilometers, it will be finished in five years. It includes the "She" Cultural Experience Area, the Recreational Health Area, an ecological agriculture sightseeing area, and a modern commercial service area, according to the standard of national 5A-level scenic spots.

In this characteristic town, She's customs and unique cultures attract people most. Phoenix is the legendary king of birds, a symbol of happiness and auspiciousness. She is the only minority who think they are descendants of the Phoenix, so each girl when married must wear "Phoenix Crown." Their marriage ceremony is like a cultural feast, creating a remarkable degree of buzz and excitement in the ancient lanes, which is welcomed by tourists who at the same time enjoy their tourist meal. The traditional marriage custom their ancestors left has been glorified as a beautiful landscape in Chinese cultural history, which prompted thousands of visitors to flock to the town to see for themselves. It brings great benefit to the local people and has led to the rapid development of the local economy.

"March 3rd" on the lunar calendar also features a well-known local activity. Every year, early in the morning the She people will gather in the Ancestral Hall, to sing songs and cook Wu rice; the place is full of bright national costumes and melodious singing. Since 2001, Jingning's "March 3rd" occasion has become the country's most distinctive national festival, and is included in China's first and second groups non-material cultural heritage by the State Council. Today, the She village between the green mountains has become a highlight of Jingning tourism.

Under She Town's construction, the Phoenix Town is the main project. It covers a 174000 square meters area approximately. With its

Qianxia Lake and traditional buildings as the cultural carrier, the Phoenix Town will be built as the traditional cultural showcase and the beautiful reception room of She Town. It integrates traditional crafts, folk arts, and delicious food. Its buildings express the town's simplicity and elegance most vividly by Chinese traditional architectures that lay the tone. Antique tiles are used to cover the roof of the building, and a lot of wood structures with small bricks adorn the facade. She ribbon elements decorate doors and windows.

The She Town also infuses culture into other kinds of elements, such as bridges and tiles. Its culture has been fully demonstrated here, which is more and more visible, audible, touchable, and appreciable in people's lives.

# 景宁畲乡小镇

早在唐永泰二年（766 年），一支在福建罗源游耕的畲族迁居浙江景宁。1000 多年来，数十个蕴含畲族风情的畲村散落在景宁，这使得景宁成为中国唯一的畲族自治县。2015 年 6 月，浙江省第一批省级特色小镇创建名单正式公布，全省 37 个小镇列入首批创建名单，景宁县畲乡小镇作为旅游产业类特色小镇上榜。小镇占地面积约 3.9 平方千米，建设面积约 1 平方千米，小镇规划了畲族风情展示体验区、休闲养生区、生态农业观光区和现代商业服务区，按照国家 5A 级旅游景区标准建设。

畲乡小镇最大的特点是风俗美。凤凰为传说中的百鸟之王，象征幸福祥瑞，直至今日，仍旧把凤型头冠作为妇女标志性装束的民族只有一支，就是畲族。畲族以凤凰为图腾，他们自认为是凤凰的传人，每位畲族姑娘结婚的时候一定要戴着凤冠行礼。祖辈留下来的畲族传统婚嫁风俗，已经成为畲乡一道靓丽的风景线。

景宁畲乡的"三月三"更是成为当地的一个著名品牌活动。每年农历"三月三"，畲族群众一大早就会云集宗祠，对唱盘歌，炊制乌饭，处处都是鲜艳的民族服饰和悠扬欢快的歌声……从 2001 年开始，景宁"三月三"已成为全国最具特色的民族节庆，被国务院列入中国第一、第二批非物质文化遗产代表名录。如今，绿水青山间的畲村风情已经成了景宁旅游的亮点，每年都有许多的游客慕名而来，带动了当地旅游业的快速发展。

凤凰古镇是畲乡小镇的主体项目，占地约174000平方米，古镇以千峡湖和畲族传统建筑为载体,将成为景宁畲族传统文化展示窗口和城市会客厅。景宁将传统工艺、曲艺、美食等民俗文化元素融入古镇建设,市井文化、民俗文化、畲族文化在此交融,建成全国知名的畲族文化街区。凤凰古镇建筑以中国传统建筑为主基调,建筑的屋顶铺设了仿古青瓦,外立面大量采用木结构和小青砖,地面以青石板铺设,建筑的门与窗融入了畲族彩带等元素,将古镇古朴雅致之气表达得淋漓尽致。

畲乡小镇还把畲族文化融入各类砖片、瓦片中去。畲族文化传承在这里得到充分践行,越来越多的畲族文化元素正以可见、可听、可触、可感的方式融入百姓生活。

# 后　记

　　法国的依云小镇靠矿泉水书写了传奇,德国的奔驰小镇让人感受到汽车工业的前世今生,美国的微软小镇独具科技城的魅力……在欧美工业化发展进程中,小城镇始终是不可或缺的一部分,许多百年、千年小镇的文化之根不但没有断裂,反而保持了其独特的魅力与活力。浙江特色小镇的建设,其灵感来源于欧美小镇。2015 年 6 月,浙江省 37 个小镇列入首批创建名单;2016 年 1 月,第二批创建名单也正式出炉,共有 42 个小镇入围。

　　浙江小镇已走在全国前列,首批特色小镇的探索已初见成效。基金小镇、梦想小镇、云栖小镇、黄酒小镇等,都有独具特色的产业和文化。小镇承载的内容虽没有大城市多,但小镇的发展却融合了城市和农村的优点,被视为中国城镇化的路径之一,有望成为联结城市和农村的新纽带。特色小镇是按"创新、协调、绿色、开放、共享发展"的理念,结合自身特质,形成"产、城、人、文"四位一体有机结合的重要功能平台。这些特色是小镇之魂,也是维持小镇生机的原动力。

　　浙江的特色小镇建设为浙江经济的发展带来了新的活力,也开创了新的县域经济发展模式。在总结自身发展经验的基础之上,将这种模式推广到全国,对于中国新型城镇化的发展、中国社会经济转型都将具有非常重大的意义。同时,通过英汉双语的形式介绍浙江特色小镇重要的经济地位、丰富的历史文化和独特的生活韵味,有助于推动中国文化"走出去",讲好中国故事,传播中国声音。

　　由于本人水平有限,加之时间仓促,本书有些英文内容显得不尽完美。鉴于此,特以中文做补充说明,并在网上搜集相关信息和图片来辅助表达,因某些信息和图片实在不明版权，如有不妥，敬请相关者多包涵。

拙著在选题、内容、版式等方面，得到了各特色小镇、浙江工商大学出版社的大力支持和帮助，在此表示衷心感谢。

王利华